NOSTRADAMUS
THE 1994 ANNUAL ALMANAC

V. J. Hewitt has devoted her working life to solving the riddle of Nostradamus's quatrains, in one of which she claimed she is actually named by the great French seer as the first – and only – person to decode his predictions accurately. She is now living in Kent, where she continues to decode the sixteenth-century prophecies, always confident of finding the answers to what our future holds.

A NOTE ABOUT THE TEXT

The completed manuscript for NOSTRADAMUS, THE 1994 ANNUAL ALMANAC was delivered to Arrow Books by V. J. Hewitt in January 1993. Since that time, the predictions have not been altered in any way.

NOSTRADAMUS
The 1994 Annual Almanac

Decoded and Interpreted by
V. J. HEWITT

ARROW

Published by Arrow Books in 1993

1 3 5 9 10 8 6 4 2

© V. J. Hewitt 1993

V. J. Hewitt has asserted her right under the
Copyright, Designs and Patents Act, 1988 to be
identified as the author of this work

First published in the United Kingdom by
Arrow Books Limited

Random House, 20 Vauxhall Bridge Road,
London, SW1V 2SA

Random House Australia (Pty) Limited
20 Alfred Street, Milsons Point, Sydney,
New South Wales 2061, Australia

Random House New Zealand Limited
18 Poland Road, Glenfield
Auckland 10, New Zealand

Random House South Africa (Pty) Limited
PO Box 337, Bergvlei, South Africa

Random House UK Limited Reg. No. 954009
ISBN 0 09 926961 9

Photoset by Deltatype Ltd, Ellesmere Port, Cheshire
Printed in Great Britain by
Cox & Wyman Ltd, Reading, Berkshire

INTRODUCTION

NOSTRADAMUS

Michel de Notredame – Nostradamus – was born on 14 December 1503 in St Remy, Provence, in France. His family was of Jewish descent, converted to Roman Catholicism, and in his teens he became a student at Avignon University.

Several years later he was discovered teaching other students that the earth was round and revolved around the sun. This contradicted the Aristotelian teachings of the Church, who had accepted for fifteen hundred years that the earth was the centre of the universe.

Fearing for his son's safety at the hands of the Inquisition, Michel's father transferred him to the medical school at Montpellier where he gained a degree in physical medicine within three years. He then set up a highly successful independent practice. In 1529 he was awarded a doctorate at Montpellier, and he lectured there before returning to his practice in 1531. He settled in Agen, where he married and fathered two children.

Only a few years later his wife and children were dead, struck down by a plague against which Michel's famed skills, for once, could not prevail. Devastated by grief and in danger once more from the Inquisition, who had summoned him to Toulouse, he fled France and wandered through Europe for nearly eight years.

It was during this period that stories of his second sight began to circulate. On one occasion, when meeting a young monk in Italy, Michel dropped to his knees in the roadway, crying, 'Your Holiness!' Many years after Michel's death, the monk became Pope Sextus V.

Michel eventually returned to Provence where he married again and settled in Salon. He wrote several books, including a compendium of home recipes for medicines, cosmetics and love potions, before publishing in 1550 the first in a series of popular almanacs. A collection of long-term prophecies set in rhyme appeared in 1555 under the title *Siècles*, or *Centuries*.

In 1556, the French queen, Catherine de Medici, summoned him to Paris to interpret one verse which seemed to predict blindness and death for her husband, Henry II. Catherine had already been warned of an identical fate for the King by an Italian astrologer. Michel had written:

> *Le lyon jeune le vieux surmontera,*
> *En champ bellique par singulier duelle,*
> *Dans cage d'or les yeux luy creuera,*
> *Deux classes vne puis mourir mort cruelle.*

I.35

> The young lion will overcome the old one,
> In a warlike field by a singular duel,
> His eyes in a cage of gold, he will blind him,
> Two classes, then one, he will die a cruel death.

The verse had been identified with Henry because the lion was his occasional emblem.

While in Paris Nostradamus (his Latin pen name) cautioned Henry and Catherine against the King taking part in any form of single combat. Three years later, Henry was killed while jousting in a tournament with Count Montgomery, the captain of his Scottish guard. Montgomery's lance had pierced Henry's eye and the King died in agony ten days later. The prophecy's 'warlike field' was in reality the tournament field. Henry had been wearing a gilded helmet with a barred visor – hence, the 'eyes in a cage of gold'. He was unhorsed in his *third* joust with Montgomery, predicted by the 'two classes, then one'.

Only then was it realised by a shocked public how closely Nostradamus' prophecy, published four years before, had described the event's vivid details, without disclosing the date, the place, or the identities of the combatants, something which would become a consistent feature of his style.

Riots broke out in Paris and although Nostradamus was once more threatened by the Church, he remained under the protection of Catherine, who visited him at Salon in 1564 with her young son, Charles IX. By this time his reputation had spread outside France, following his further prophecies of the death of Henry's son, Francis II, in 1560, and the return of Francis' widow, Mary Queen of Scots, to her own kingdom.

Nostradamus suffered for some years of the condition known as 'dropsy' and was found dead on the morning of 2 July 1566, having correctly predicted that his body would be found between his bed and the bench he used to climb into it. In 1568, a collection of 942 of his prophecies was published. The prophecies were translated into English at the beginning of this century and interest in them has become worldwide.

Because there is a lack of connecting detail to place his prophecies firmly within an historical framework, many of his detractors have stated they were merely a brilliant, but meaningless illusion, despite the fact that Nostradamus once wrote that he had 'twisted' his original, clear predictions into their present form to prevent his generation from seeing the future.

So many dramatic changes would soon befall humankind, he reasoned, that the men of his time would not understand them until they had actually happened. So his prophecies, muddled and apparently capable of many different interpretations, have always had to wait for events to catch up with them.

That has remained the case until this decade.

NOSTRADAMUS UNRAVELLED

My work decoding the prophecies of Nostradamus has been published throughout the world.

For twelve years I have studied his writings, convinced that their mystical language disguises a logical, consistent method of understanding them. I am now satisfied that Nostradamus deliberately designed his verses to resemble distorted prophecies with the intention of keeping his readers fascinated for several centuries. This 'great illusion' enabled his work to survive into a more rational age, with the means of deciphering them being concealed within the verses themselves. My theory is that each verse is a linguistic device, capable of generating many hundreds of predictions.

Through intense research of his text and style, I have developed a system, using a consistent set of rules, of extracting clear predictions from the original prophecies. When this decoding system is applied, each prophecy becomes a four-line puzzle whose component letters can be constantly reassembled to present accurate, dated predictions concerning any subject.

What this means in practice is that I have become totally free to dictate the subject and starting point in time of each prediction independently of the original prophetic verse. I believe this was the fundamental intention of Nostradamus – that his system could one day be used to explore the future without, necessarily, his close involvement. (Although in predictions using the 'I' form I believe that his intensely personal vision of the future is being offered to us.) A single, essential link remains: that between his original verse puzzles, and the decoding system to which they have been designed to 'respond' in producing numerous predictions for our own age.

In today's civilisation, prophecy, if it is even seriously considered, is viewed as a fleeting, unreliable phenomenon. But with the decoding system, it can become a precise instrument for probing the development of human society in any direction – scientific, religious, ecological, social.

The availability to this generation of such a device, as we move into a new millennium, has tremendous implications. Our huge, complex society is forced to be reactive in the absence of accurate predictions. We can only stir ourselves into action once a situation is established fact, by which time it is already too late. The accelerated pollution of the world's environment and the rapid increase of the elderly as a proportion of Western populations are two prime examples.

Now, as we journey towards the obstacles and challenges of not just a new century, but a new millennium, we have the means to help us plan our route. This, I believe, was the ultimate goal of Nostradamus, in constant danger of torture and hideous death at the stake, writing his prophecies over four centuries ago.

The next millennium promises to be so different to this one, in terms of knowledge, belief and character, that we need a strong bridge to cross the chasm.

In the work of Nostradamus we may have discovered that bridge.

DECODING THE PREDICTIONS

Nostradamus wrote his prophecies as quatrains: four-line, alternate rhyming couplets. They appear in ten numbered 'centuries', or sections of 100 verses each, with the exception of 'Century Seven' which contains forty-two. The muddled, incoherent style of the text is based on old French, with a sprinkling of other languages.

As a French doctor and astrologer of Jewish descent living in the sixteenth century, the age of increasing Protestantism and the exploration of the Americas, Nostradamus was extremely modern in his outlook. But he was also heir to an ancient, mystical and philosophical tradition: the Jewish Kabbala, which regarded words and numbers as vehicles of prophecy. Words were 'shells' concealing other words, other meanings. In the same way, numbers could also transmute, one into another. Nostradamus assimilated this knowledge into the writing of his prophecies.

Consequently, instead of interpreting the prophecies of Nostradamus as they were written, I treat each one as a 'super-anagram'.

Anagrams are the key to using the prophecies to predict the future. How do anagrams work? On a much more simplistic level, let's use the word 'live':

LIVE = EVIL = VEIL

Here, I've simply moved the letters round to make two new words which are solutions to the source word, *live*.

Take another word – *antagonism*. How many words are hidden there? *Ant* is obvious. Change it a little and you get *tan*. Move on and you spot *tag*. But other words are not immediately visible. You have to work a little to extract words like: *mist*, *stigma*, *moan*, *most*, *tin*, *gismo*, *gist*, *gin*, *mango*, *Saigon*, *tango*, *smog*, *togs*, *tongs*, among others.

All of the letters in each word can be found in the source word, *antagonism*, which acts as a concealing 'shell'.

Then there are words containing one letter that is *not* present in *antagonism*: for instance, *stage*, *game*, *sage*, *agonise*.

Each of these words contains the letter 'E' – but there is no 'E' in *antagonism*. All their other letters can still be found in the original word. Using this method you could begin to compose lists that are hundreds, even thousands, of words long.

Suppose that you do not have a word or a phrase, but a sentence totalling 20–30 words with a fair sprinkling of most, if not all, the letters of the alphabet. From this sentence compose a list of all the words, phrases and, finally, sentences you can think of, using both precise (words with all the letters matching) and imprecise (words containing one letter that is different) solutions.

It is impossible to guess how many items you would end up with. The number is probably infinite, or as close to infinity as we can comprehend. Each time you changed the subject – drew out the letters of that subject from the sentence – you would change the groupings of letters that remained. These remaining groupings of letters would provide the new back-up sentence about your subject.

And that, essentially, is how the Nostradamus decoding system works.

Selecting Predictions

When I planned this book, I decided to focus on a single year – 1994 – with the aim of returning to the form in which Nostradamus originally published his predictions; the almanac of 1550. I chose, as my prediction 'generator' the aptly numbered Prophecy 9.94.

Next I drew up a list of all the subjects on which I required predictions: the poor, babies, Yugoslavia, South Africa, John Major, the United Nations, the European parliament, the Loch Ness monster, archaeology, physics, computing . . . In the following pages you will find predictions on all these subjects and many more.

One question which always crops up is: How do you know that there's a prediction in the prophecy about Margaret Thatcher, or Michael Heseltine, or Princess Anne, if it doesn't contain these particular names?

The answer is that there is *always* a prediction, because the system works automatically. The name of the subject is extracted, letter by letter, from the original prophecy. The letters and syllables that remain conceal, in anagrammatic forms, the prediction about that subject.

The Numerical Code

The French text of the decoded predictions is expressed through a twenty-four letter alphabet. Each letter of this alphabet has its own numerical value. The numerical values combine to produce the dating:

a	b	c	d	e	f	g	h	i	j	l	m
1	2	3	4	5	6	7	8	1:9	10	11	12

n	o	p	q	r	s	t	u	v	x	y	z
13	14	15	16	17	18	19	20	21	22	23	24

'K' and 'W' can also be present in the text, but they have no numerical value. The letter 'I' has two values – the Roman I and the Arabic 9.

The first step is to 'enter' the specific period for which I require predictions – in this case 1994. Since any prophecy can generate predictions for any time period, the fact that I have chosen Prophecy 9.94 is not enough. The system has to be 'instructed' to predict only for a certain year.

The experimental mechanism, or 'time key', for this is the withdrawing of three letters that correspond to the numerical values, t–i–d/19–9–4, from the prophecy before any further decoding takes place. This 'advises' the prophecy that it is now in the year 1994. This withdrawal of t–i–d must take place before the decoding of any prediction required for 1994.

Let's choose a subject – say, the grand overview of Britain in 1994. What are the most important features of our country's destiny in that year? This is the original prophecy, couched in Nostradamus' extremely individualistic style:

> *Foibles galleres seront unies ensemble,*
> *Ennemis faux le plus fort en rampart,*
> *Faibles assailles Vratislaue tremble,*
> *Lubecq et Mysne tiendront barbare part.*

IX.94

This is where my approach differs radically from that of other interpreters of Nostradamus. It would be usual to offer a translation at this point. However, if this verse is *designed* only to resemble a *distorted* prophecy – as I assert – then it would be useless to attempt to interpret what is an illusion. Indeed, it is necessary to forget that these look like words and phrases at all! What we actually see are cleverly assembled groups of letters, nothing more. These groups have, in reality, been combined to form a device of formidable prophetic power. The date and content of the series of predictions emerging from this device are directed by the 'time key', in this case t–i–d, or 1994, and the subject which, in this example, is *la Grande Bretagne dans cette année*.

Tid – la Grande Bretagne dans cette année . . .

1994 – Great Britain in this year . . .

Some letters cannot be found in the original verse (the three overlined) and these will eventually be linked with another letter drawn from the verse. When you withdraw the letters making up a) the dating mechanism and b) the subject from the prophecy, what is left?

> Fo ll s s o u i s s m b l e
> E emis f ux le plus for en r mp r
> F ibles assailles Vra   islaue tremble,
> Lube q et Mysne tien ront barbare part.

These remaining letters conceal the prediction for the subject during the year 1994. Here is my solution:

tid – la Grande Bretagne, dans cette année je vois la constitution barrée assaillie de toutes parts, le peuple sulfureux, les remaniements frêles; or la réforme.

1994 – Great Britain, in this year I see the blocked constitution attacked from all sides, the people sulphurous, the flimsy reshuffles; now the reform.

If you are new to these predictions, you may be astonished by the force and clarity of this statement – the voice of Nostradamus himself, resonating through his own creation. Here, in an encapsulated form, are the key features for 1994: the perceived faults of constitution and government, a resentful British people and the panicky, superficial responses of the Conservative administration to social unrest and widespread demand for change on a scale not witnessed in living memory. The prediction ends with the promise of reform on the horizon.

The new prediction leaves fourteen letters remaining from the 'box of letters' in the original prophecy. These fourteen letters from the prophecy are those placed above the following text, with the 'new' or inserted letters immediately below.

```
        f     b   s              m
tid – la Grande Bretagne, dans cette année je vois la
b                    l   l       b           q
constitution barrée assaillie de toutes parts, le peuple
     m              y   s   b   b
sulfureux, les remaniements frêles; or la réforme.
```

Together, the 'old' and 'new' letters combine to form the dating system, drawn from the numerical alphabet we discussed on page 6.

I arrived at the principles behind this solution and others like it after twelve years of research. For me, the process of detecting hidden ideas and constructions is, by now, almost spontaneous. (Conversely, I now find it very difficult indeed to explain each individual step, because this requires the slowing down of the mental process to a crawl in order to be able to explain it.) Having used this method for so many years, I also know much more about the predicted future, which helps me a great deal.

Dating the Predictions

```
f b s  m  b  l  l   b  q  m  y  s  b b
d g d  j  c  d  o   t  e  u  t  e  o e

6 2 18 12 2 11 11  2 16 12 23 18  2 2 = 56        = 11
4 7  4 10 3  4 14 19  5 20 19  5 14 5 = 79 = 16 =  7
            5 10        2 10      5
```

The upper row of numbers equals the days of the month; the lower row, the months themselves. Some two-digit numbers are added together to produce the month number as on the third row here. From left to right, dates are 6 April (F = 6; D = 4 [the fourth month]), 2 July, 18 April, and so on.

Each set of dates relates to the section of the text from which it springs. Therefore, analysis of each section produces a month-by-month interpretation of the predicted event and its impact upon the year 1994.

Each prediction also has a single main date focusing on one of several aspects of a predicted situation – its beginning, its most intense point, the moment when a vital decision is taken or implemented, or the time when its momentum begins to fade. Here, the main date is 11:7, or 11 July. In this book, the main date for the predictions from January to December 1994 appears on the top right page of each prediction.

The dating is often expressed in periods of time. So events predicted may not begin or end with each main date, but there should be some indication at that point that the situation described is being 'activated' in real time.

The same dates often recur in different predictions and I have two theories for this. First, the art of numerology teaches us that the numbers one to ten are related to different aspects of existence. Therefore, the same dates (made up from such numbers) may always be connected with the same types of events.

Furthermore, I have noticed that certain dates coincide with major astrological conjunctions; however, I have not pursued this aspect since I am not a professional astrologer and Nostradamus issued a famous warning to all astrologers to keep away from his prophecies, despite the fact that they are littered with astrological references. Long ago, I took this to mean that astrology was not the key to understanding his texts.

My aim in producing this almanac is to demonstrate that many predictions can be extracted from a single original quatrain. Therefore, although I have offered this detailed explanation of how I decode a prediction, all evidence of decoding has been stripped away from the remaining predictions in this book. What matters here is variety and quantity.

All the predictions were decoded between March and August 1992. Each prediction was decoded using the steps outlined above. The dating and interpretations were produced between the months of August and December 1992.

I translate the French predictions literally. In my view this is necessary, because a more *graceful* translation might lose essential elements of the meaning. This is especially relevant when I go on to create the interpretations from a section-by-section analysis of each prediction.

In 1991 I published fifty predictions for the period 1991–2001*. Because of the timescale, many of these have yet to be fulfilled, but accurate predictions so far include:

China's isolation, following the disintegration of the Soviet Union (1991).

The formation of the Commonwealth of Independent States following the Soviet collapse (1991).

The decision to move the capital of Germany from Bonn to Berlin (1991).

The first visit by ex-King Michael to Romania since being deposed by the Communists after the Second World War (1992).

Early signs of recession in the Japanese economy (1992).

Vote to ordain women priests in the Church of England (1992).

Predicted breakthroughs during the 1990s in gene therapy for a variety of diseases are also well advanced, as is a prediction of multi-racial elections in South Africa for 1994.

My work is seen as a revolutionary approach to the work of Nostradamus, and has not been easily accepted. Such acceptance will only happen if large numbers of these predictions come true. Indeed, if they are to be fulfilled, what we will witness during the remainder of 1993 and on into 1994 are rapid changes in every aspect of society 'permitting' these predictions to come true.

Since what I do is decode within a defined system, without possessing the all-embracing vision of the true prophet, I am always limited by the amount of information I can extract from each prediction. I accept that I am vulnerable to criticism unless and until each prediction is fulfilled. Nevertheless, my twelve years of using this method have convinced me that it provides an informative, precise way of knowing what our future holds. In the world's present difficulties such a mechanism has never been more needed.

I am sufficiently encouraged by the success of this method so far as to hope that these predictions will be of value to many who read them.

V. J. Hewitt
January 1993

* Nostradamus – The End of the Millennium.

THE WORLD IN 1994

GREAT BRITAIN

In 1994, only six years away from the new millennium, Britain will confront a rapidly changing and turbulent world. Old certainties will no longer exist. Nationalism and religion will vie with each other as international issues.

Britain will confront great difficulties within the domestic economy and encounter a chaotic, often violent, scene at home and abroad. Far from receding, the severe economic recession will deepen to a point where everything hibernates. Financial institutions, in particular the High Street banks and building societies, will struggle against a rising tide of bad debt.

The social conscience issues rise near the top of the political agenda, as poverty and unemployment become increasingly linked to the incidence of crime. In this year there may be civil unrest as political protest finds no outlet in the present system of government. Many political issues are fuelled by resentment and passionate debate, such as the campaign for Scottish independence. The health service, education and environment all fall under the spotlight. Drought in many areas of Britain will become an emotive issue throughout the year.

An underlying public unease with many areas of government will make itself felt by the end of the year in widespread demands for constitutional and political reform.

John Major remains Prime Minister, but famous faces come and go. In parliament 'frenzied politics' produce fierce reactions from a Conservative government at bay. Margaret Thatcher and David Owen prepare to re-enter the political arena.

The times reflect the 'turbulence' always experienced at the approach of a new millennium. Nowhere is this more felt than in politics, with a Conservative party divided from January to December. The government faces a difficult, volatile year, full of crises and the need for swift decisions. Much government action may be reactive. Important realignments on the Left and the Right are in the air.

Animal rights will become an explosive international issue,

with protests ranging from tourist boycotts to more extreme forms of action.

This book is being completed at the end of 1992 when the monarchy under Elizabeth II has just passed through a very difficult year. Nostradamus predicts that Prince Charles will become King in the very near future. Despite their separation announced in December 1992, Diana is also predicted to become Queen.

In 1994 the monarchy is troubled and may seem unresponsive to demands for reform. King Charles will be seen as a remote figure, taking up issues which do not touch the lives of ordinary folk, while the image of Queen Diana assumes a 'cult' status, overshadowing the institution of the monarchy. Prince William will become a public figure in his own right during this year.

NORTH AMERICA

All of Nostradamus' predictions show a sudden and severe decline in America's fortunes, resulting from natural and economic disaster. This period begins in 1993.

The effect of this disaster on Europe will be particularly disruptive, since America will withdraw from any form of foreign policy in order to deal with problems at home. American finance for European projects and organisations may begin to dry up.

Many Americans will flock to Britain and Europe to renew their careers, particularly in the film industry. Social order in the United States will be under severe strain all year, while Canada also finds herself dealing with the overspill of America's problems.

EUROPE

World attention will be focused on Europe this year as a continent divided for 1500 years since the fall of Rome struggles to forge an indivisible alliance. The withdrawal of the United Nations from any part of European affairs will make this action necessary.

The on-going civil war in former Yugoslavia accelerates public anxiety when conflict also breaks out between neighbouring Greece and Turkey. Albania and Italy are drawn into the maelstrom.

In the absence of leadership from the UN and America, the European Community will be forced to mount a massive military campaign in Yugoslavia. British forces, including the Gurkhas, will distinguish themselves in this operation.

Forming a backdrop to all European domestic and foreign

policy is the realisation that the United States is no longer in a position to exert any foreign influence.

Europe has it within her to become a single superstate, a stabilising influence in a changing world. In 1994 the political signs show that, however unwillingly the prospect is viewed, a new self-governing European Community will emerge out of the need for many nations, including those presently outside the community, to act together. Never has Dickinson's adage: 'by uniting we stand, by dividing we fall' been more apt.

Europe will be the hope of a deeply troubled world.

MIDDLE EAST

Egypt and her neighbours, stirred up by environmental crisis, will become resentful of Western indifference. Iraq joins other Arab nations as they begin to draw a net around Israel.

FAR EAST

China will begin a long revolution for democratic reform, while relations grow tense between India and Pakistan.

AFRICA

Nelson Mandela may become President of South Africa. Elsewhere on the continent, famine and strife march together as before.

SCIENCE AND TECHNOLOGY

If there is one area where blessings abound it is in the realm of science. Theories and discoveries flash across the spectrum like so many comets.

Astonishing medical treatments grow apace. Technology may begin to enable the blind to see and the deaf to hear. Scientific advances promise to turn the tide against ecological pollution.

Satellite broadcasting and revolutionary new techniques in computing herald a world full of scientific 'toys' which reach the consumer as never before.

The discovery of the holy grail of the scientific world – nuclear fusion – is predicted for 1994, holding out the prospect of clean and endless supplies of energy. Nuclear power stations using the process of fission will eventually become obsolete.

A voyage to Mars becomes a real possibility.

Startling medical evidence emerges that paranormal activity is a natural function of the brain. A period of intense scientific research into psychic activity will begin.

RELIGION

At the end of 1994 the Church of England will be exhausted after a long period of internal strife. The Church will become engaged in urgent talks with representatives of Islam, possibly in connection with tension in the Middle East. Many scientific discoveries during the year will be seen as a threat to traditional religion. Believers will find their faith shaken by the questions being put forward and reaction could temporarily set in against scientists investigating the basic matter of life itself.

These predictions do not gloss over the difficulties that Britain, Europe and the world will face in 1994. Nor should they, for if we have an inaccurate map, how can we hope to explore our future safely?

Knowing already of the fascinating changes coming to Britain and Europe later in the decade, I would characterise 1994 as 'the darkest hour before the dawn'. The rest of the world will take a little longer to set to rights.

LIST OF PREDICTIONS

JANUARY

**Industrial waste – New Laws ● Queen Diana
Calms the Mob ● Europe Debates Rights of
British Poor ● Winter Snow Threatens Homeless**

INDUSTRIAL WASTE – NEW LAWS

Les compagnies que font dèchet industriel doivent télécopier un bureau à détail. Il y a règlements larges sur l'enlèvement barré. Ballast en sas de parlement.

Companies that produce industrial waste must fax an agency in detail. There are sweeping regulations over prohibited disposal. Ballast in the sieve of parliament.

The government may introduce this Act in a tough political year when the Houses of Commons and Lords will be angrily divided. The law is 'ballast', keeping the government afloat in stormy waters, and it receives widespread support.

From 2 March Parliament discusses the bill and companies strenuously lobby MPs (6 March to 17 April).

Around 18 March it emerges that companies proposing to dispose of waste must notify in detail an official agency. Divided groups will unite to support the bill during 1 April to 17 May. Between 2 and 18 April details of waste to be disposed are agreed –possibly by type, category, quantity, method and site of disposal.

During 18 April to 18 May the official agency and its responsibilities will be defined. Around 2 May the agency acquires the right to regulate and prohibit disposal.

Between 12 and 18 July further sweeping measures may be announced. The government may rush through this bill to become law at the end of July.

From 6 August all industrial waste is subject to the new act.

In October (2, 17 and 22), perhaps at the party conference, the government stresses its environmental concern, using this new law as an example.

QUEEN DIANA CALMS THE MOB

Reine Diana tient une place d'honneur du suprème degré aux yeux des gens qui savent terreur seule. Sans police pacifie tôt les fomentateurs dans les rues.

Queen Diana holds a place of honour of the highest degree in the eyes of people who know only terror. Without the police she soon calms the agitators in the streets.

Queen Diana, held in high public esteem, devotes ever more time to visiting tragic outcasts who live in desperate conditions, as well as promoting charities to help them.

The prediction may be describing a particular incident around 8 January. Separated from police bodyguards, the Queen finds herself confronted by a mob on the streets, who, when she is recognised, allow her to pass unmolested.

More likely, this reflects a continuing trend in which she dispenses with such protection in order to work more freely among people who live with different terrors every day – hunger, cold, violence, authority and, inevitably, fear of dying.

Between 2 April and 15 June, Diana's work may be recognised in an official capacity, perhaps as head of a new foundation to aid the homeless, or she may be nominated for an award or honour. Special recognition may come on 6 August.

During early February and again on 11 May and 2 July, severe outbreaks of unrest may occur, which Queen Diana may help to bring to an end with direct appeals in dangerous circumstances.

A further incident may occur on 2 October.

EUROPE DEBATES RIGHTS OF BRITISH POOR

En l'Europe on se met finement les droits des pauvres britanniques sur l'ordre du jour politique. On refuse l'argument comme fallacieux. Résulte à la misère.

In Europe the rights of the British poor are cleverly manoeuvred onto the political agenda. The argument is rejected as fallacious. It results in misery.

Eighth of January focuses on the plight of Britain's poor. A prediction illustrating one in many examples of the power Europe will begin to wield over Britain's domestic affairs.

The day on which these rights, or the lack of them, are first debated appears to be 10 January, but arguments for increasing aid to the poor are rejected as false, presumably by the British government.

At first, this may be solely a domestic issue, since it is not until 6 February that the coding gives it a European dimension. Later on in the month (18), the 'manoeuvres' are successful in having this aired in a European forum.

Between 1 and 11 April, the issue may be intensely debated in the councils of Europe, with possible royal intervention in the form of speeches, or charity work, occurring during 1 and 18 May. Royal personages may be accused of interfering in politics.

Between 2 July and 19 August extreme problems could be experienced by those on low income levels (perhaps connected with predictions of drought and violence in a hot summer).

A strong movement may arise to better their conditions, persuasively arguing (2 to 18 October) either to the British government, or, more controversially, to Europe, in an attempt to gain intervention, so bypassing parliament.

Nevertheless, circumstances may not significantly alter for poor people in 1994.

WINTER SNOW THREATENS HOMELESS

Aux premiers trois mois de l'an, le temps enneigé déguise la faute de l'eau. On couvre les fêlures. Lamentablement la froideur taille ce qui sont sans foyer.

In the first three months of the year, the snowy weather disguises the lack of water. The cracks are covered. Deplorably, the coldness prunes those who are homeless.

'Winter' extends across 21 December 1993 to 20 March 1994. The important date is 13 January, although 2 to 13 February also appears to be a 'beacon' period, with the first heralding the effects of low temperatures on the homeless and the second signifying the onset of the severest winter weather with spells of intense cold.

Britain's ongoing drought, an increasingly emotive public concern throughout 1994, is disguised during the winter by heavy falls of snow. Severe weather may continue until 2 April.

Some of those who die on the streets from the cold and combined effects of homelessness may not be discovered until 15 March when the snow begins to clear, or be cleared.

Between 1 April and 2 to 18 May, the effects of long-term drought may become visible as the snow and cold fully recede and the cracked dry earth becomes fully visible for the first time in months.

A significant development, perhaps a report on the plight of the homeless, or a debate in parliament, could be expected around 17 to 19 May.

A climax to this process may occur during 1 and 17 October.

FEBRUARY

Government Rejects American Need for Aid • Virtual Reality Sparks off the Paranormal • Cost Threatens Nuclear Deterrent • American Stars Flock to Britain

GOVERNMENT REJECTS AMERICAN NEED FOR AID

*Le gouvernement britannique exprime soupçons sans fonde-
ment qu'on n'a pas besoin d'assistance à l'Amerique, malgré la
mysère manifeste. On ne le relève pas.*

The British government voices groundless suspicions
that aid is not needed by America; despite the obvious
distress, it is ignored.

Nostradamus has foreseen a decade of natural and climatic
disaster for America, beginning in 1993.

In 1994, America's need for aid will be the focus of intense
debate, especially within the European Community. Around 6
February, appeals for aid, perhaps by individual states, may be
made. The American government could swallow its pride and
sanction these requests.

Between 6 May and 6 December the British government may
oppose the sending of aid, arguing that America's huge physical
and social resources do not need more help. Britain's own serious
economic situation may be a factor.

Second of April is important, while 'groundless suspicions' are
linked with the period between 11 April and 11 May. The
government, despite the obvious distress of the American people,
may attempt to deflect a growing international accord.

During 18 March to 11 May, other countries may listen to
Britain's arguments, ignoring America's distress until the significant period between 17 April and 13 June. The situation is
suddenly reversed (2 July) as it becomes apparent that America
cannot cope with her massive problems (17 to 19 July). This
development may be linked with rising public concern, sparked
off by television and press reports.

Eleventh of October indicates a change of heart by the
government. A cynical observer of politics would note that it
occurs during the annual party conference season!

VIRTUAL REALITY SPARKS OFF THE PARANORMAL

On croit que les machines que produisent virtual reality mènent les gosses en influence néfaste, mais par effet latéral stimule paranormalité latente.

The belief is that machines that produce virtual reality have a bad influence on youngsters, but through a side-effect it stimulates latent paranormality.

By 1994 virtual reality technology will be as familiar as karaoke machines.

Technology consists of a headset and goggles, worn with a sensitised glove. Armed with these, the player can enter a computer-generated world where he or she can explore any area on Earth and fantastic games worlds, walk on the surface of the Moon or even dance on a star.

Its huge fascination for young people may attract criticism, but not immediately understood is the fact that this technology will stimulate an area in the brain, dormant in most of us, that produces paranormal activity. People who use it for long periods may become psychic. From 2 February the first evidence that this is happening, either here or abroad, could emerge.

Between 2 April and 11 May the conviction that youngsters are wasting their time will increase. The second of July may see an official decision or action which affects the machines around 22 August.

During 2 to 18 October, scientific evidence could emerge that virtual reality technology stimulates paranormal activity in the brain. Because the prediction does not refer to a specific country, this is probably an international development.

This prediction may alarm many readers, but in later years scientific investigation into psychic ability will lead to astonishing and beneficial developments in controlling powers of the mind.

COST THREATENS NUCLEAR DETERRENT

La glorification de l'arme nucléaire de dissuasion britannique cesse quand on ne peut pas remplir la sébile. Ses veterans défenseurs essayent de barrer.

The glorification of the British nuclear deterrent stops when the begging bowl cannot be filled up. Its veteran defenders try to obstruct.

The Conservative government retains an independent nuclear deterrent, but from 10 February the cost begins to weigh heavily in comparison to other demands on the economy.

America's own plight, highlighted earlier, may have much to do with this. Indeed, America's refusal to fund parts of European defence could prompt scrapping of the deterrent. The money is needed elsewhere. A unified European defence policy may emerge as Europe is forced to make many decisions without America. Alternatively, the 'begging bowl' may be Britain's own, since predictions also highlight the dire state of her economy.

During the period between 11 February and 2 April, a consensus may grow in favour of abolishing the deterrent. Nineteenth March is significant.

When the danger to Britain's deterrent becomes clear (between 12 March and 19 May), there will be fierce opposition.

From 12 September to 11 October the Right wing of the Conservative party may belatedly press for reconsideration of the decision.

A linked event may occur on 2 October, but the prediction does not say whether or not the attempt to change government policy is successful.

AMERICAN FILM STARS FLOCK TO BRITAIN

Le brasier modifie la vie future en fulgurante vitesse. Une galerie des stars americains voyage à la Grande-Bretagne par tenir roles opposés en les films.

The inferno alters the future outlook with lightning speed. A gallery of American stars travels to Great Britain to act in contrasting film roles.

A lack of work – caused by natural and economic catastrophe predicted for California and Hollywood – could drive American actors, producers and directors to Europe. The prospect beckons of making films for a huge, European audience that soon will surpass the current American market.

By 6 January, many Hollywood stars will be without work. Eleventh February could signify a widespread realisation that they will have to look to Europe.

Between 2 and 12 March, one-way traffic to Britain may begin, with stars setting up residence, organising finances and creating production companies.

During 2 to 22 April, they find an almost non-existent British film industry and many European governments fiercely protective of their own film cultures. Nevertheless, American films are hugely popular with European audiences and much good will may exist.

Between 2 and 13 May many stars accept film roles very different from the characters they usually play. Some may produce, direct or do other unfamiliar jobs.

Around the period between 2 and 11 July, a further influx could alter the British film industry with lightning speed.

Between 16 and 19 July, and 12 August, studios and production companies could be set up in Britain, where technical expertise in making films is second to none.

A flourishing 'base' is in place with the promise of many new jobs by 11 October.

MARCH

Reluctant Europe Adopts UN Role • Babies
Proved Psychic Before Birth • Heseltine Replaces
Lamont • Virginia Bottomley out of Government?
• Insolvency Threatens Building Societies •
Michael Caine – A New Hit Film • Harriet
Harman – Law on Child Benefit

RELUCTANT EUROPE ADOPTS UN ROLE

L'Organisation des Nations Unies n'affronte pas toutes les exigences du monde. Il faut que l'Europe devient responsable de ses bords, or les membres ralent.

The United Nations organisation cannot cope with all the problems of the world. It is necessary for Europe to take responsibility for its own borders, but the members grumble about it.

From 12 February, the UN secretary general and other leading voices may urge that Europe shoulders responsibility for dealing with increasingly chaotic and dangerous situations within her own borders. This call may, at first, be ignored by European leaders.

During 1 and 17 April, the UN may withdraw from any European responsibility. Members of the EC may complain, but from now on the United Nations will direct its attention to other matters on the world stage.

Between 1 and 23 May the European Community begins to adopt a much more positive, even assertive, role to disputes between member states – whether or not those states object. Top of the list will be Yugoslavia.

Second of July signals a period of great difficulty.

During the period between 1 and 17 September, membership of the EC may be extended to nations in Central and Eastern Europe. From 2 October, the community may be moving towards closer political union as a buffer against the acceleration of international events.

BABIES PROVED PSYCHIC BEFORE BIRTH

À la médecine le foetus fait preuve de sensible à toutes sorts de cas arrivant au loin. Semble qu'il est psychique à gré. Le plus des enfants oublie à naissance.

In medicine, the foetus proves to be sensitive to all sorts of events happening at a distance. Apparently, it is psychic at will. Most children forget at birth.

This is a prediction with profound implications for society, science and human belief. Around 11 to 17 February tests establish what the baby in the womb knows about events outside the mother's body. The notion that the foetus is cocooned from such knowledge is swiftly dispelled.

From 17 February to 12 March, experiments test these theories. During the period from 2 to 17 March reactions of the foetus could be measured. Random samples of outside events, not known to the mother, could be mixed in with the tests. Reactions of the foetus show that it is aware of these external factors.

Tests on newborn babies reveal that most have 'forgotten' this extra-sensory ability – the trauma of the birth process desensitising the receptive area of the brain. Some retain awareness. They react to events happening at a distance. In other words, they are psychic.

Between 17 July and 2 August the scientific world reluctantly admits that psychics exist. True psychics exercise their ability at will. Fleeting psychic experience (dreaming of future events, or having a 'hunch' that something is going to happen) is random low-level activity exercised by the numbed 'psychic' area of the brain.

Between 2 and 12 September, and 17 October, psychics demonstrate varied abilities, as well as sensitivity to distant events and stimuli.

During the period between 6 and 13 October, experiments determine whether or not this ability weakens over considerable distance. Planet-wide tests may take place.

GOVERNMENT HEADS FOR DISASTER

*En une période de politique affolée, Major mène le gouverne-
ment vers un désastre. Il faut stabiliser. Norman Lamont part,
remplacé par Michael Heseltine.*

In a period of frenzied politics, Major leads the government towards disaster. It must be stabilised. Norman
Lamont leaves, replaced by Michael Heseltine.

In 1992 Norman Lamont is the Chancellor of the Exchequer. If he
holds the same position in 1994, then Michael Heseltine will
become the new chancellor in a government reshuffle at a time of
political crisis for John Major.
The 'disaster' has two aspects, the first beginning on 18
January, touching on 11 March, and concluding or climaxing on
18 March.
A second nemesis for the government arrives within the time
frame of 2 to 19 April, not easing until after 6 June. During this
period of 'frenzied politics' the government will be making
desperate manoeuvres. Important dates are 2 and 18 to 22 May.
Norman Lamont's position may be uncertain from 2 March, but
his replacement is predicted to begin between 1 and 17 August.
This could mean that Heseltine may not immediately replace him
('frenzied politics', indeed, with three chancellors in one year!),
or, more likely, that he achieves a high public profile at that point.
The government 'has to be stabilised' around 11 October,
indicating a strong effort to keep grass roots supporters on side for
the annual party conference. Much political excitement may be
concentrated on Lady Thatcher (see page 156).

N.B. Norman Lamont left the government in May 1993. In June,
Michael Heseltine suffered a heart attack which has left him out of
politics for several months. We must wait for events in 1994 to sort
out this contradiction!

VIRGINIA BOTTOMLEY OUT OF GOVERNMENT?

Au printemps – à la session de parlement le ministre Virginia Bottomley se trouve au milieu de colèriques députés où ils sassent alarme génerale des gens.

Spring – in the parliamentary session the minister Virginia Bottomley finds herself among easily angered back-benchers where they sift the general alarm of the people.

Virginia Bottomley, in 1992 Secretary of State for Health, is 'reshuffled' at the same time as Norman Lamont – around 13 March.

Her position may be uncertain from 2 January to 6 February. In the Commons she may experience attacks from backbenchers reflecting disquiet from their constituents. During the period from 11 February to 2 March, this note of alarm sounds most clearly.

Protests and even demonstrations may be expected around 1 April.

From 22 April to 6 June, parliament will be confused and angry. Further important dates are 6 and 13 May.

By 11 April, Mrs Bottomley could find herself one of a number of backbench MPs attacking government policy. The Conservative party will become increasingly divided. Public anger may make itself felt from 17 April to 2 May.

Demonstrations and protest could take place between 1 and 17 July.

Virginia Bottomley moves into the limelight again between 2 September and 6 October. On 2 October she may express her own disquiet and those of others on official policy, while on 11 October she could become the focus of widespread criticism or party division.

These divisions may come to a head at the annual party conference.

INSOLVENCY THREATENS BUILDING SOCIETIES

Le prix des maisons continue à tomber. Les ventes sont tres lentes en les faubourgs; or la perte faramineuse ménace les sociétés immobilières en faillite.

The price of houses continues to fall. Sales are very slow in the suburbs; now astronomical loss threatens the building societies with insolvency.

From 1 to 17 March, events make it increasingly clear that building societies will face calamitous financial losses during 1994.

The slump in the British housing market will have witnessed many thousands of homeowners having their properties repossessed, while takings from new mortgage holders and savers continue to plummet.

Consequently, all building societies will face a very difficult year and some will have to deal with the prospect of ceasing business altogether.

From 11 April to 2 May, house sales may pick up a little, but the improvement is shortlived. By 17 May the suburbs, where sales have fluctuated, will provide little or no activity for estate agents.

By 11 to 23 September, sales will be so low that during the period from 6 to 17 October, many societies will be battling to save themselves from going under.

After 2 October, their losses will be 'astronomical', and as a result some societies are bankrupted.

Such a development may occur on 11 December.

MICHAEL CAINE – A NEW HIT FILM

Acteur anglais Michael Caine fait un effet saisissant avec un film au sujet d'un homme blessé par une bombe paquet destiné au patron. Excluré, il se revolte.

The English actor Michael Caine makes a striking impact in a film about a man wounded by a parcel bomb intended for his employer. Dismissed, he rebels.

The main prediction is clear enough, but Michael Caine may not be the first choice for this film. Between 17 January and 18 February, work could start on the production, which then runs into difficulties. During the period of 14 to 17 March the actor originally playing the role may leave or be fired.

Around 18 March Michael Caine could take over the part in difficult circumstances.

During the next three months (2 April to 2 June) film production runs smoothly.

Between 18 and 23 August Caine could be injured in some way during filming, although this injury does not appear to be serious.

Between 5 and 17 October, he is making headlines, perhaps in connection with the film, but certainly reaching a high peak of success in his career. It is possible that he could accept a part at this time in another production with a very 'English' theme.

HARRIET HARMAN – LAW ON CHILD BENEFIT

Le député Harriet Harman pilote un loi par le parlement des passés d'armes que fait obligatoire de lever le niveau d'allocation d'enfant. Une montée énorme.

The MP Harriet Harman pilots a law through parliament, amid heated exchanges, that makes it compulsory to raise the level of child benefit. An enormous increase.

Around 17 March the Labour Shadow Minister, Harriet Harman, may announce a bill which would compulsorily raise the amount of child benefit.

Child benefit was 'frozen' for a time during the Thatcher government and has never regained its former value in real terms. Such a bill, if passed, would certainly impose an enormous increase.

Verbal exchanges on the subject may occur on 18 January, with preparation up to 2 March, when a specific proposal may be announced.

By 2 April, Harriet Harman may be spearheading a campaign, including this bill, to promote child welfare in Britain. Debate follows on 17 to 18 April, and 18 May.

By 2 May, a bill could have been introduced in parliament. During 6 to 18 June, it may be making its way through the House of Commons or Lords.

During the summer Harriet Harman could achieve much publicity. After 2 October the bill may become law. Further important dates are 6 and 23 of that month.

Such an act could not be passed without the votes of rebel Conservative backbenchers. They will have an eye to their constituents, who will view the government with deep disdain.

APRIL

Split Support Helps Liberal Democrats ●
European Parliament – A New Supremacy ●
European Troops Partition Yugoslavia ● Danger
to Ocean Floor Explorers ● Debt-ridden Banks Hit
Business ● Yeti Tracks in the Snow? ● South
Africa – Whites Elect President Mandela ● Philip
Schofield organises Aid to America ● A Dry
Spring – Water Shortage Grows ● Football –
Row Over Commercialism ● New Laser
Treatments for Rare Diseases ● Lack of Sex
Education Kills ● Germany, France, Libya in
Crisis ● Tourists Shun Whaling Countries ●
Corrupt Justice Stirs Public Anger ● Michael
Crawford – the Definitive *Phantom* ● Michael
Palin – Prize-winning Director

SPLIT SUPPORT HELPS LIBERAL DEMOCRATS

*Les Démocrates Liberaux et Labour offrent la sélection fêlée.
Ashdown saisit le basse en soutien par barrer bien les Conservateurs en parlement. Gains.*

The Liberal Democrat and Labour parties offer a split
choice. Ashdown seizes on the drop in support by
expertly obstructing the Conservatives in parliament.
Gains.

Nineteen ninety-four holds out the possibility of a decisive
realignment on the Left following a gain in public support for the
Liberal Democrats, splitting voter choice between them and
Labour.

From 6 February, the Liberal Democrats' appeal could be
translated into the winning of by-elections in Conservative-held
seats between 2 March and 2 April.

By 11 March, public support could be evenly divided between
the main two opposition parties – a development that Labour,
endeavouring not to lose a fifth consecutive general election,
would naturally view with alarm.

During the period between 12 and 15 April, Paddy Ashdown
could be negotiating with Labour to form a coalition for the
European parliamentary elections due to be held in 1994.

Between 11 and 23 May the two parties could act together,
offering a single candidate in each constituency to maximise
votes. The Conservatives could lose seats.

Eleventh of August sees Paddy Ashdown making news, while on
16 October he may seize an opportunity connected with a very
difficult situation developing in the Conservative party.

EUROPEAN PARLIAMENT – A NEW SUPREMACY

Le parlement européen devient presque autonome, sitôt que la commission de Bruxelles assied son autorité – temps barbare. Il faut abandonner Strasbourg.

The European parliament becomes almost autonomous, as soon as the commission at Brussels establishes its authority – savage times. It is necessary to abandon Strasbourg.

Why does this massive shift in the power of the European parliament become necessary? These are indeed 'savage times', with war clouds gathering in the Middle East, civil war in Yugoslavia and conflict between Turkey and Greece, ostensibly over Cyprus, but probably complicated by widespread Balkan hostilities involving the Muslim population. Albania is also involved and the entire region seems likely to become inflamed.

America, with its own all-consuming domestic problems, cannot or will not aid Europe.

Many have argued that at the heart of the Maastricht Treaty was a vacuum where a federal European government accountable to a federal European parliament ought to have been. Here, we see the first forced steps towards such a destiny.

Decisions granting independence to the European parliament may arise around 5 February and over the years it will have to achieve the status of a sovereign parliament, if Europe is not to disintegrate altogether.

One of the less publicised decisions of the Edinburgh summit between EC leaders at the end of 1992 was the permanent location of the European parliament in Strasbourg, despite the fact that the parliament is set to move into a brand new building in Brussels in 1993. However, from 1 April 1994 it will become necessary to abandon Strasbourg and concentrate all activity upon Brussels. This may be effected or decided upon by 17 May and could be one of the first decisions made by the authority of the new parliament.

During the months of April and May quick decisions will compel the European commission to abandon responsibility in most areas. A new administrative civil service responsible to the European parliament may emerge from 6 to 11 April, and 6 May.

By 23 April, the parliament's responsibilities may be defined, with almost full autonomy recognised for it by 14 May.

Between May and June, the parliament will have to establish its authority against domestic dissension and grave foreign conflicts – including a massive European military operation in Yugoslavia; important dates are 11, 18 May and 2 June.

That process strengthens during 16 July.

By 2 to 6 October the new parliament may be sitting in full session. On 19 October all necessary measures to govern Europe may be in place.

The importance of this prediction for Europe's future wellbeing cannot be overestimated. The 1994 European elections are the key.

EUROPEAN TROOPS PARTITION YUGOSLAVIA

La Yougoslavie – les nations de l'Europe usent les troupes à morceler Bosnie, Croatie et Serbie. Séparent les barbares, l'un de l'autre, las, batailleur, sans fer.

Yugoslavia – the European nations use troops to partition Bosnia, Croatia and Serbia. They separate the barbarians, one from the other, weary, aggressive, without iron.

After several years of civil war between peoples of the old Yugoslavia, the European Community will take the decision to send in a military force made up of troops from several European countries.

This and other predictions indicate that the operation will be massive, with British troops heavily engaged for much of the time. Because of her recent experience in fighting the Falkland and Gulf Wars, it is likely that Britain will be in overall command.

Throughout the time between 2 January to 13 February the civil war could be fading, with all combatants wearied, although sporadic outbreaks of fighting may still occur.

Around 12 March the situation may suddenly worsen. A new conflict could break out between Croatia and Serbia. During 6 April to 12 May, the war will gradually engulf all the regions of the old Yugoslavia and may threaten to spread beyond its borders.

At this point (8 April) the European Community decides that it can no longer stand by, or restrict its activities to guarding aid convoys. Force must be implemented. The intention will be to bring an end to the fighting, and to establish neutral land corridors between each region. Such an operation to separate 'the barbarians', as Nostradamus calls these fierce peoples, may be planned, or begin, between 12 April and 16 May.

By 6 May, European troops could be present in force in Bosnia. Around 12 May an operation to separate this region from others may begin, or be active.

Around 2 August, fighting could be bitter and intense, the most difficult part of the conflict.

By 22 September, it is possible that an end to the war could be in sight, but a total end to the fighting may not come until after the end of the year.

This prediction must be read in context with others surrounding events in this volatile region where conflict threatens to involve Greece, Turkey, Albania, as well as the Middle East.

The potential danger to the community is probably the main reason why the European parliament suddenly achieves a new supremacy on the same day (see page 00).

Circumstances necessitate the formation of a sovereign European parliament to oversee the course of a protracted and bitter struggle. In the new Europe no other body will have the authority to make such decisions on behalf of the community.

The prediction gives no hint of an American involvement. Nor is it likely, in light of current American circumstances, that there will be any. This will be purely a European operation, the first within her own borders since the Second World War and the first by a European alliance anywhere without American involvement since Suez in 1956.

DANGER TO OCEAN FLOOR EXPLORERS

L'exploration des mers use un nouvel vaisseau à traverser bel fond sous-marin. Apres le départ, en bref minute, les courants ménacent à saisir les voyageurs.

The exploration of seas uses a new vessel to cross the beautiful ocean floor. Following departure, in a brief moment, the currents threaten to seize the travellers.

New technology in the form of a vessel that travels across the sea floor may make underwater exploration easier, but the idea still sounds dangerous. The vessel holds at least two people, who are able to see a strange and beautiful world as it moves across the sea bed. Pressures at such depths will be enormous.

The dangerous currents that seize the vessel could occur in early trials during January to March. The problem is evident on 1 January, again on 5 February, and may continue throughout the time between 19 February to 2 March.

However, difficulties are gradually overcome and, by 11 March, the prospect of using the vessel to explore the sea bed becomes much stronger.

By 12 to 14 April we may see the first serious 'walk'. Between 6 April and 2 May, explorative trials increase, while from 11 April to 11 May, views of the sea bed filmed from the vessel may be shown to the public at the first time.

During this period, the vessel may have been operated by remote control, or have contained one intrepid 'test pilot', but from 19 May at least two people will operate the vessel.

During the week of 2 to 8 August, serious preparations will be in hand for extended sea trials, and on 5 to 6 September, the vessel may set out on its first long journey.

Bon voyage!

DEBT-RIDDEN BANKS HIT BUSINESS

À la Grande-Bretagne les banques principaux amassent mauvaises créances énormes. On demande frais de banque à prix fou des entrepreneurs. Total hiberne.

In Great Britain the main banks pile up enormous bad debts. Business people are asked to pay bank charges at an exorbitant rate. Everything hibernates.

From 2, 11 and 19 January the High Street banks, having accumulated massive bad debts, may give notice of increased charges to business.

During 11 February to 11 March the scale of bad debts being written off by the banks becomes clear. The date 6 March is important.

During April, particularly 11th, the situation worsens, with extreme difficulties presenting an unfortunate outlook for the banks.

Between 11 and 18 to 19 April, the banks may announce a large rise in bank charges and these could begin to have a deleterious effect on business enterprise during 2, 12 to 23 June when business people may protest loudly at what they perceive to be the 'madness' of exorbitant charges.

During the period between 6 and 18 July and on to 19 August, the main banks may be faced with a considerable loss of business, as their customers increasingly look to foreign banks for financial backing and investment.

Meanwhile, the British economy has slowed down to a state of virtual 'hibernation'.

YETI TRACKS IN THE SNOW?

Le yeti des Himalayas – des ascensionnistes trouvent traces étranges sur la neige. Elles les mènent jusqu'a leur odorat les informent d'animal près. Départ.

The Himalayan yeti – some climbers find strange tracks in the snow. They follow them until their sense of smell informs them of an animal nearby. Departure.

This prediction appears to describe a single incident at a particular time, and it may well do so, but analysis of the dating reveals a more complex situation.

Between 2 January and 11 February an expedition may be mounted to prove the existence of the Himalayan yeti. Over many years, climbers have seen footprints, heard strange cries and even witnessed this creature of Tibetan legend, a large walking ape or hominid.

During 6 March and 6 to 22 April, the expedition may come across the creature's tracks. On 11 April they come close enough to detect the pungent scent of a yeti.

During 5 April to 12 May information about the creature's way of life may be gathered, but contact with a single animal or group could be lost around 17 April.

Persistence for the next two weeks may pay off, however, for it is around 2 May that climbers could sight at least two females of the species.

Between 6 July, and 2 August to 2 September, there could be constant sightings throughout the Himalayas, or a complete lack of sightings. The prediction is not clear.

During the month between 2 September and 2 October, familiarity with a group of these animals could enable study at first hand. On 6 October, an odd incident could occur. Five days later there may be a close encounter between human and yeti.

SOUTH AFRICA – WHITES ELECT PRESIDENT MANDELA

Les gens blancs votent tièdement pour fort Nelson Mandela à devenir Président d'Afrique du Sud. Le procés du scrutin de ballottage sasse les sieurs paumés.

The white people vote half-heartedly for the strong man Nelson Mandela to become president of South Africa. The process of a second ballot sifts the lost masters.

Between 1 and 12 February, white politics still hold sway in South Africa, but by March the white electorate is voting, but without much enthusiasm, for what it sees as inevitable political change.

The process may occur in two parts, with whites voting in the first period for a new constitution permitting black South Africans to vote and hold public office.

During the period between 17 March and 17 May, a second ballot may be held to elect the new president of South Africa. From 2 April to 12 May, Nelson Mandela could become the new president of South Africa.

The rest of the prediction appears to concern the white citizens, now a minority of the South African electorate, who feel increasingly powerless and adrift in a period of accelerated change.

This latter period extends across 17 June, 6 July and 5 to 22 September, and may present problems for the new president.

Note that this prediction does not refer to citizens in South Africa who already have the vote but only to the whites. Their decision is the key to a new future for the country.

PHILLIP SCHOFIELD ORGANISES AID TO AMERICA

La Grande-Bretagne – l'acteur Philip Schofield soude en bref temps une force européenne au but d'envoyer à trame l'aide à l'Amerique, à la bète folle en liberté.

Great Britain – the actor Phillip Schofield welds together in a short time a European organisation with the aim of sending through a network aid to America, to the crazy animal in the wild.

This prediction takes place against the government's refusal to join in sending European aid to America. On 13 February, an unofficial aid scheme organised by showbusiness personalities may begin to be co-ordinated.

By 18 March, the organisation may be up and running.

Between 12 April and 18 May, a network of contacts is forged. On 18 April a press conference may launch an appeal with the intention of sending aid by 11 May.

Setbacks may occur on 2 May, and again between 17 and 18 May when aid convoys may be in danger from armed looters in America.

Those who cannot accept the American situation, as described in this prediction, should know that Nostradamus has frequently prophesied a series of catastrophes for the United States. Without exception, his forecasts all echo the same tragic trend for the rest of the decade.

By 15 June, European countries scramble to add their efforts to the aid network.

On 12 July our European partners may go ahead with official aid, but without Britain. British aid organisations may be thrown back on their own resources.

Between 18 and 22 August Phillip Schofield could be involved with transporting aid to America – obviously an activity carrying some danger due to civil disorder. Known as a children's TV presenter and the lead in *Joseph and the Amazing Technicolour Dreamcoat*, he may now have adopted a permanent acting career.

N.B. The prediction decodes his first name as 'Philip', although it is spelt 'Phillip'.

A DRY SPRING – WATER SHORTAGE GROWS

Au printemps britannique, il fait le temps très sèc. On fore des puits à trouver l'eau, mais fentes en sol et l'affaissement sont rebelles à barrage meilleur.

In the British spring, the weather is very dry. Wells are sunk to find water, but cracks in the ground and subsidence are resistant to improved damming.

The spring period relates to 21 March to 20 June. As early as 11 February, plans may be formulated to sink many new wells or to locate other forms of fresh water supplies. This development indicates growing official and public alarm about the state of Britain's water supply system and the effect of the encroaching drought.

The British spring, notwithstanding predicted heavy falls of snow in the winter just past, provides little or no rain. The drought and its effects may begin to emerge as an important public issue.

Between 2 and 4 April many projects to sink wells may be started – water diviners may find themselves in demand as never before!

Coming to June, serious efforts will be in hand to improve the containment and damming of all water supplies, from the domestic network to reservoirs. The fact that twenty-five per cent of all water is lost through leakage in the system may be of relevance. Many wells are sunk during this period.

By October, the lack of rainfall noticeable in spring will continue and deep cracks begin to appear in terrain which would normally be moist from autumn mist and rain.

FOOTBALL – ROW OVER COMMERCIALISM

Angleterre – en sus de la Première Ligue, le football produit l'esprit commerçant que règne partout. On fait une raison valable au système, mais le sérieux va.

England – as well as the Premier League, football produces a spirit of commercialism that prevails throughout. A legitimate case is made, but genuineness disappears.

Reforms of the game, acts of parliament regulating the safety of grounds, hooliganism and the emergence of the Premier League have all combined to produce years of disturbance for the average English fan who loves football.

1994 promises to be no exception.

Between 2 February and 2 March unpopular reforms or measures, resulting from commercial pressures, may be introduced which for many will spell the end of football as they see it.

Between 11 and 12 February, and 18 March, the genuine article is sacrificed to the spirit of commercialism pervading the national team by 13 April and spreading to English regions between 18 April and 18 May.

Between 2 and 5 May vigorous protests, or even a court case, could thrash out the issues. The football authorities appear to win, because these new reforms are in place throughout the Premier League and probably the rest of English football by 2 July.

The Premier League will be making news around 6 October, but setbacks may occur between 13 and 18 October as unsuspected faults emerge in the recently introduced commercial measures.

NEW LASER TREATMENTS FOR RARE DISEASES

Technologie nouvelle à laser comprend usage à fréquents multiples d'une fibrillation fixe en traitements des certaines maladies rares. Elles partent.

New laser technology includes the multi-purpose use of a fixed fibrillation in the treatments of certain rare diseases. They leave.

As in this case, it is sometimes possible to decode a prediction for a subject about which I have no practical knowledge. Nevertheless, I hope that this one means *something* to those who work with lasers in medicine.

During 2 March 1994, a deeper understanding of certain rare diseases may be reached. This understanding develops until 18 April.

Between 11 April and 2 May this research is linked with fibrillation, which, in medical terms, refers to an uncontrollable twitch or spasm in muscle tissue, or, more specifically, in the wall of the heart.

Around 17 April these new ideas may be focused on developing laser technology to treat certain medical conditions. The technology may assume its new form after 2 May and be in use from 18 July.

By 2 to 18 October the new technique undergoes experimentation in a variety of ways and trials could occur during 12 to 23.

These early trials may soon be an overwhelming success with the complete elimination of at least one of the conditions between 17 October and 1 November.

LACK OF SEX EDUCATION KILLS

L'éducation sexuelle en lycées britannique – on la tient à être trop grosse pour beaucoup d'enseignement. En attendant, la mort a sabré le boisage malavisé.

Sex education in British schools is considered to be too coarse for much teaching. Meanwhile, death has cut down the ill-advised saplings.

In January 1994 the sexually transmitted disease AIDS may be speading among Britain's schoolchildren, with the numbers of deaths increasing, although a report or information admitting this may not become public knowledge until 11 February to 18 March. The date 2 March is significant in that it may emerge that numbers of HIV cases in schools have risen sharply.

Nevertheless, the government, educational authorities and, most of all, boards of school governors, may attempt to eliminate all but the minimal biological facts about sex from the education curriculum. This situation may intensify around 2 to 18 April, with, perhaps, some public speeches or debates on the issue.

Between 6 April and 6 May, sex education in schools may be severely restricted, perhaps by legal means.

During 11 to 12 May the campaign against sex education in schools may reach new heights and a restrictive ban on all but the plain biological facts may be in force by 17 to 18 July.

Around 11 October, new facts may come to light demonstrating that the campaign against sex education is ill-advised. Schoolchildren are now contracting the HIV virus in increasing numbers without the knowledge of how to protect themselves against infection.

It is difficult to discuss a predicted situation without knowing all the factors involved, but it is possible that the incidence of mothers who have infected their offspring with the HIV virus may be much higher than is supposed. Teenagers nowadays become sexually active much earlier and, without adequate education, those who are HIV positive could endanger other pupils. Other possibilities could include infection from blood transfusions carried out during the early nineteen-eighties.

GERMANY, FRANCE, LIBYA IN CRISIS

Allemagne serré d'une sérieuse crise économique, pendant qu'en parts de la France les immigrés Arabes numérotent un tiers. Tôt la salve balafre Libye fât.

Germany gripped by a serious economic crisis, while in parts of France Arab immigrants number a third. Soon, the volley of shots gashes conceited Libya.

This prediction focuses on three separate countries – Germany, France, Libya – apparently locked together in a violent economic crisis.

During 2 to 15 January, the leader of Libya, who may or may not be Colonel Gadaffi at this point, could become the subject of an assassination attempt. If so, it appears likely that this attempt will not succeed.

An uprising, or civil war, may follow with many Libyan Arabs fleeing beyond their country's borders to Western Europe, particularly France and Germany.

The spotlight then switches to France where, between 18 February and 2 April, a third of the population in some areas could now be Arab immigrants from several countries, including Libya. Important dates are 2 to 11 March and 11 April.

During the time between 6 April and 22 May, Germany is also gripped by a crisis, particularly around 18 April; this crisis is connected with what is going on elsewhere.

On 11 May the situation appears to be exacerbated by the increasingly large population of Arabs in France and, perhaps, parts of Germany (18 July).

TOURISTS SHUN WHALING COUNTRIES

La pèche à la baleine par excés fait réclamations indignées. On emploie le tourisme terne comme une sanction. La lutte blesse les pays. Les ravages cessent.

Whaling to excess produces an outcry. Lacklustre tourism is used as a sanction. The struggle wounds the countries. The ravages stop.

From 17 January, countries still operating whaling fleets, despite international pressure, may be ravaging certain species of whales to extinction.

Public speeches point out (2 to 17 March and 16 April) that a boycott by tourists could forcefully bring it home to the governments of these countries that whaling is ultimately unprofitable. Tourism is potentially the world's biggest international money-maker.

Between 6 March and 7 April there may be a public outcry against whaling nations.

Remonstrations are not enough, nor is the threat of withholding tourism from these countries since it will not be taken seriously. The international public comes to understand that it must take concerted action to avert disaster for the whale.

During the weeks between 17 April and 2 May, public feeling begins to bite. Tourists choose holidays elsewhere, while stating why they have taken 'strike action'.

Between 2 and 17 May and 2 June, a significant drop in the numbers of tourists could begin to hit national economies, a vital factor in a continuing world recession.

During 17 July, 20 August and 6 October those countries that still hunt the whale have been deeply affected. As a result, whaling will soon cease.

CORRUPT JUSTICE STIRS PUBLIC ANGER

La Grande-Bretagne – l'administration des cours de justice est si mauvaise qu'elle blesse le britannique. La magistrature fausse sème notion de la réforme.

Great Britain – the administration of the courts of justice is so wrong that it offends the British subject. The false judiciary spread the idea of reform.

In recent years miscarriages of justice have come to light, shaking public confidence in the English legal system. Distrust of the judiciary deepens in 1994.

Between 11 and 15 January a form of justice, perhaps a legal decision, or evidence given in a case, is universally viewed as false by 2 February.

This causes much public debate during March and April, being closely linked with the administration of courts of justice. Important dates are 11 March, and 2, 6, 15 April.

During 15 to 17 April the issue so offends the public notion of justice and fair play that efforts to bring about reforms may begin around 17 May.

Throughout July, particularly on 6, 13 and 16, judges are mainly on the defensive, although some may have become convinced of the need for reform.

By 2 to 11 October the situation has intensified, perhaps because of the intransigence of the judges, spreading the view that tinkering with the system is not enough and fundamental reform, amounting almost to a revolution, is required.

On 22 and 23 October support intensifies for constitutional reforms that secure rights of access to information for British citizens.

MICHAEL CRAWFORD – THE DEFINITIVE
PHANTOM

Au film 'Phantom of the Opera' l'acteur anglais Michael Crawford fait une telle interprétation sensible du défiguré qu'elle devient l'emblème permanent.

In the film *Phantom of the Opera* the English actor Michael Crawford creates such a sensitive interpretation of the disfigured one that it becomes the permanent emblem.

Early in the year, between 2 and 18 February, intense publicity surrounds a woman in the film.

Around 18 March, attention focuses on the actor Michael Crawford, who had a stunning success in Andrew Lloyd Webber's famous musical with his stage portrayal in London and America of 'the Phantom'. He will also play the role in the film. Clearly, it will be a memorable, sensitive performance.

Between 2 and 18 April publicity may concentrate on his ability to play 'the disfigured one' who is also psychologically disfigured. Crawford may be giving interviews, or early reviews of the film could be rapturous.

Between 18 May and 18 June, the album of music from the film could possibly be released.

From 18 July to 18 August, Michael Crawford may spend some time in France, perhaps in Paris, since the story is set there.

Around 22 August he may have returned to promote *Phantom* in a special event.

The film will go on general release in the UK after a première attended, no doubt, by members of the Royal Family. The build-up for 2 October is intense, with reviews and articles extolling Michael Crawford's portrayal of the Phantom.

Around 1 December he may receive or be nominated for an award.

MICHAEL PALIN – PRIZE-WINNING DIRECTOR

L'acteur anglais Michael Palin réalise un film que gagnera beaucoup de prix, d'un fomentateur. Il trouve à mystère des vestiges sérieuses d'Allemagne Nazi.

The English actor Michael Palin directs a film about an agitator, that will win a great many awards. He finds in mysterious circumstances some genuine relics of Nazi Germany.

Michael Palin, of 'Monty Python' fame, recently made a great impact in the Channel Four political drama 'GBH', while also fulfilling his dream of travelling round the world and making highly successful television series about it.

A number of possibilities are implied about a film which Palin will direct, perhaps winning many awards, although dating suggests a different scenario. Between 2 and 19 January a 'mystery' comes to light, perhaps the germ of the idea for the film.

Between 5 and 18 February, Michael Palin could be setting up the financial aspects, while from 2 to 13 March he could decide to play a leading role, as well as directing the film. Sixth March is important.

In April he may be honoured for previous work.

During 2 to 19 June and 6 to 17 July the focus may switch to Germany. An English actor, perhaps not Palin, could win the role of a Nazi in the film. He may replace someone else. There could be German political objections to the venture.

Meanwhile, the spotlight falls on the 'relics'. Negotiations could occur to secure genuine Nazi items for the film and permission may be secured by 2 October.

Between 14 and 18 October Michael Palin may begin directing the film, which could be controversial.

MAY

Bruno Fights for World Title ● Alternative
Medicine Under Threat ● African Refugees Flood
Rome ● Man vs Animals – Brain Holds Secret ●
Human Evolution – An Exciting Theory ● Animal
Inspection – Treasury Rejects Cost ● Ministers
Resign in Sex Scandal ● Homeless Win Right to
Housing

BRUNO FIGHTS FOR WORLD TITLE

Le boxeur Frank Bruno essaye de gagner le championnat du monde. En la mêlée porte un coup au tête de son adversaire qui a la fibre sensible. Bruno fer se tient.

The boxer Frank Bruno attempts to win the world championship. In the mêlée he strikes a blow at the head of his opponent who is susceptible. Iron Bruno contains himself.

Frank Bruno has fought twice before for a world title, once against Mike Tyson when he was stopped in the fifth round. This time he may have a better chance.

February 1 to 11 sees Bruno in the peak of condition and dedicated to his goal of becoming a world champion. Eleventh March may create an impact.

During 2 to 19 April negotiations which receive worldwide publicity could be taking place. Bruno's opponent is not named, but appears to be dominant so it is possible that he is world champion already; this is not an elimination fight.

The date 5 May is important, perhaps signifying a sealed contract.

During 6 to 18 May there is enormous publicity and some confusion surrounding the forthcoming match. Attention is focused on what might be Bruno's last attempt to win a world title.

The period 18 July to 11 August could see Bruno in winning style.

ALTERNATIVE MEDICINE UNDER THREAT

Les ostéopathes, ménacés des lois européens, resserrent à l'union
aux practiciens de médecine alternative. Le gouvernement fait
lui barrer. Ne réussit pas.

Osteopaths, threatened by European laws, join forces
with practitioners of alternative medicine. The British
government acts to prevent it. It does not succeed.

Alternative medicine in Britain, from acupuncture and herbal
medicines to crystal therapy, is a multi-million-pound industry.
Laws originating from Europe will threaten to restrict or even
abolish sections of this thriving industry.

Between 11 February and 11 March the medical world may join
in public discussion of such proposed action, which may involve
an added workload for GPs. Between 12 March and 2 April, GPs,
realising this, may join vigorously in the debate.

Orthodox medicine could also find itself regulated by Europe, a
prospect which it would probably resist strenuously. The views of
the British government will weigh into the debate (6 to 16 March
and 6 April). The row may focus on a directive, or perhaps a bill to
be introduced in parliament, from around 2 April.

Resistance grows in April and May. Practitioners of orthodox
and alternative medicine could join forces with European
counterparts (11 April to 11 May) to fight regulations imposed by
European law-makers.

Between 2 April and 2 May, the government could act to
prevent such an association, but will not succeed. The association
will be active by 1 June. Around 6 August, osteopaths, until now
aloof, could join in protests at regulations also directed at them.

Laws could be in force by 2 October, with further regulations
introduced by 11 to 12, and 23 October.

AFRICAN REFUGEES FLOOD ROME

Rome – point de non-retour sonné. Rumeurs abondent. Le pape lassé Jean Paul II meséstime effet retentissant des africains affamés qui arrivent sur mer basse.

Rome past the point of no return. Rumours abound. The exhausted Pope John Paul II underestimates the lasting effect of Africans who arrive starving over a low tide.

Rome and the Vatican will face a chaotic period. Vast numbers of refugees from Africa will be arriving in an overwhelmed Rome, after a personal initiative from Pope John Paul II. The Vatican itself may shelter many of them. The 'low' tide refers to the inland sea of the Mediterranean.

The refugees may be Arabs from North Africa, fleeing from conflict, but numbers may be swelled by escapees from famine and political disorder elsewhere in the continent.

The Pope's welcome may not be echoed by many Romans because normal life in the capital is hindered. Numbers arriving make it impossible for everyday life in the city to continue.

Refugees begin arriving between 23 February and 2 March. They effect a permanent change to the city, evident between 2 and 11 April. The date 7 April is important to Rome.

Between 11 April and 11 May rumours may focus on the Pope's health, though denied by the Vatican between 2 and 5 May.

Around 2 June Pope John Paul may issue an edict or otherwise use his authority to quell unrest in the city, but by 2 September his reputation may be so low that he could be the target of open ridicule.

After 11 October, this mood could intensify into resentment by Romans who regard him as having made too many mistakes. Enforced repatriation could begin.

MAN vs ANIMALS – BRAIN HOLDS SECRET

L'investigation du cerveau revèle les cellules que tiennent la différence entre l'homme et les animaux. Sape en masse l'orgueil à notre espèce rassemblée.

Investigation of the brain reveals the cells that hold the difference between man and the animals. It undermines to a great extent pride in our collective species.

Research of the human brain reveals a factor within certain cells that accounts for the different intellectual capacities of humans and animals.

The discovery has an unexpected effect. Many people realise how much we have in common with animals and how much we can learn from them. In years to come, the balance of power between humans and animals may be altered.

This tiny difference may first be established around 2 to 6 March. Discoveries about different species could follow between 17 and 18 March, although nothing may be published until 2 April.

By 17 April attention focuses on our debt to our animal heritage, conflicting with deeply held beliefs that we are separate and 'higher' than animals. Confusion intensifies from 1 to 2 May, when religious belief could itself be threatened. During the period between 17 and 19 May an argument arises that we are no more than clever animals. Everything we do can be explained by our animal inheritance.

Resistance may begin around 6 to 18 July, with further scientific investigations throughout the rest of the year attempting to prove the discovery wrong and to restore the pre-eminence of man over creation.

The period 18 August to 15 October could signify public calls to renew pride in the unique qualities of humans.

HUMAN EVOLUTION – AN EXCITING THEORY

L'étude d'homme ancien fait une théorie que galvanise le monde scientifique et les medias. Le larynx a developpé par besoin sur de barboter à mer basse salée.

The study of ancient man produces a theory that galvanises the scientific world and the media. The larynx has evolved from a definite need to paddle about in a low salt tide.

Similar predictions often 'cluster' round the same point on the calendar, as if some invisible stimulus activates changes that are related. May reveals what we are and where we came from.

This prediction recalls the 'aquatic ape theory', which proposes that our ape ancestor became semi-aquatic for one to three million years in Africa, before returning to land. This 'long swim' resulted in our walking on two legs, loss of body hair and our ability to swim and dive, together with many other anatomical features which separate us from our nearest relatives, the great apes.

With the discovery of ancient human fossils around 11 March, the world is galvanised until 18 April by the impact of a major find that could provide answers to these and many other questions about human evolution.

The period between 6 and 18 April focuses on the larynx in the fossils, which are possibly located by the shores of an ancient sea. From 13 April the media may latch on to the implications of this find.

Between 19 April and 2 May theories abound. The larynx has developed for a definite purpose, other than speech, coinciding with a period spent 'paddling in a low salt tide'. Could this be a reference to the Mediterranean? Theories fly until 17 to 19 May.

After 18 May, one theory may emerge from all the rest – it includes the development of speech and could be published during 11 August to 6 October. By 17 to 18 October most of the scientific world have accepted it.

ANIMAL INSPECTION – TREASURY REJECTS COST

À la communauté européenne on inspecte exactement le transport des animaux vivants à l'abattage. Le fisc britannique refuse à rembourser les frais à loi.

In the European Community the transport of live animals for slaughter is strictly inspected. The British Treasury refuses to reimburse the compulsory payment.

The prediction does not say *why* the British government refuses to pay. Disagreement may arise over regulations imposed by the European Community, or British farmers could object to sharing the cost.

Transport of live animals to the Continent for slaughter could continue during 1 January to 5 February, although the Treasury may at this point refuse to pay the inspection costs.

Between 11 March and 2 April the whole issue of transporting live animals could come to the fore. This could mean that British animals are banned from being transported live unless inspection costs are paid for, or that they are transported without any official inspection made at all.

The period between 11 March and 18 April could see questions raised about the quality of inspection and the legality of certain actions.

Between 23 March and 18 April the British Treasury and the government may be in direct conflict with the European Community over this issue.

By 2 to 18 October, it could be arranged for animals to be slaughtered in the UK and their carcasses transported to the Continent, thereby avoiding the need for the government to reimburse live animal inspection payments.

MINISTERS RESIGN IN SEX SCANDAL

Les nouvelles, le part fabriqué, éclatent d'un scandale sexuel au gouvernement où ministres donnent ses démissions à Major. Il est baissé au mauvais temps.

News, partly invented, breaks of a sex scandal in the government where ministers tender their resignations to Major. He is weakened at the worst time.

Two months after a wide-ranging reshuffle of government by John Major, disaster strikes in the form of a scandal in which more than one minister is predicted to resign. The facts may be 'partly invented', but there is a sufficiently large grain of truth to make the rest seem plausible.

Around 10 January the spotlight focuses on John Major, criticised for leading a weak government.

Between 2 February and 2 March attention will focus on the government reshuffle already predicted for March, played out against serious international events. By 17 March, the reshuffle is complete.

One month later, around 17 April, the government finds itself in deep trouble, with an impending scandal which might not yet have broken in the media. Other reasons for the resignations may be presented to John Major. He is 'weakened at the worst time' because of the government's involvement in plans for a massive European military intervention in Yugoslavia.

The real reason for the resignation may break in the press around 6 May, but could produce little impact at the time because international events are making all the headlines.

Later in the year, when the Conservative party is hotly divided, the press may again fasten on this scandal with scathing comment. An important speech affecting John Major could be made around 6 October.

HOMELESS WIN RIGHT TO HOUSING

Il semble que, par loi européenne, personnes sans foyer à Grande-Bretagne ont droit à logement aux installations de lavage et cuisine – or un bref semestre.

It appears that, under European law, homeless people in Great Britain have a right to housing with washing and cooking facilities – now a brief six months.

Between 6 and 11 April all homeless people within the European Community will win the right to be housed by their respective governments. The standards of a civilised society are not compatible with people living rough.

During the week between 11 and 18 April and on 11 May this right may become controversial when applied to the British homeless.

Directives to speed up this process may be issued between 18 April and 12 May. A huge operation follows, with lists of all empty houses and their current state of repair, while a return to council-house building or the prefab, so popular after the Second World War, might be on the cards.

Although the government may resist from 17 April, a time limit of six months from 1 May could be imposed to house every homeless person. From 2 May preparations on a national scale may get underway. Further regulations may be issued between 6 and 18 May, to become effective later in the year.

Between 2 and 11 July all housing provided will have to possess adequate facilities for bathing and washing clothes, including, of course, the connection of the water supply.

Between 2 and 11 October, cooking facilities must also be provided.

These last two points suggest that the British government may be dragging its heels over providing basic facilities in houses allocated to homeless people.

JUNE

Labour Woos Liberal Democrats ● Woman
Attacked by Wild Panther ● Sean Connery
Chooses Scottish Politics ● Channel Tunnel –
Strange Experiences ● Space – The Dream of
Mars ● Air Traffic Controllers Strike ● Britain
Breaks with Commonwealth ● Israel – Isolated
Among Enemies ● Nile Fails – Europe Scorns
Egypt ● Cannabis Legalised ● Turkey and Greece
War Over Cyprus ● Nuclear Fusion Will
Transform Europe ● Exile Agassi Faces Lawsuit

LABOUR WOOS LIBERAL DEMOCRATS

La Grande-Bretagne – le parti de Labour réalise qu'il a besoin de secours des Démocrates Liberaux. Tempère la passion de débat. Tout le temps la bannie brèche.

Great Britain – the Labour Party realises that it needs the help of the Liberal Democrats. It moderates the passion of debate. All the while, the woman exile breaches . . .

Despite the government's continuing problems, Labour will have difficulty in offering itself as the only alternative to the Conservatives, because of a surge in Liberal Democrat support at the beginning of 1994. Between 12 and 18 January, the Labour leadership may realise that Labour cannot win by itself.

Between 12 March and 18 April this belief strengthens. After 21 March their help may be actively sought by Labour in a pact or coalition, perhaps for the 1994 election to the European parliament – a crucial time for all Europe.

An important date for Labour and Britain is 6 April.

During the next few weeks, Labour cools 'the passion of debate' with the Liberal Democrats in the hope of political gain. Vital dates are 12 to 23 April, 11 to 18 May and 13 June.

The 'woman exile' could be Baroness Thatcher – exiled from the Commons while constantly attacking government policy. She may make an important statement after the European parliamentary elections.

Around 6 July Britain in Europe could become a subject of headlines and speeches, while on 17 August a political barrier is breached.

By 11 October, Margaret Thatcher could be considering an important political decision (see page 156).

WOMAN ATTACKED BY WILD PANTHER

Les animaux sauvages errent par la Grande-Bretagne. À l'ordinaire, on ne les voit jamais, or un chat grand, peut-être une panthère, assaille une femme. Bête lèsé.

Wild beasts roam about Great Britain. Usually they are never seen, but a big cat, possibly a panther, attacks a woman. The animal injures . . .

Unknown to most Britons, colonies of exotic wild animals, birds and spiders – mostly escapees from zoos and private collections – are flourishing in our countryside.

Numerous sightings have occurred for years of 'big cats' and the time between 6 and 23 January 1994 will be no exception. In a cold, snowy winter many animals are seen, including large cats, but no attack takes place.

A further sighting of a large cat may occur on 11 February and again on 18 March.

In April debate focuses on whether this is a large domestic cat, or a cross with a Scottish wild cat, but later in the month the belief grows that it is one of the great cats.

Between 18 April and 2 May, a woman may be injured by an unknown animal, though tell-tale wounds indicate a member of the cat family. *Bête lèsé* could also mean that the animal itself is injured and unable to hunt, which is why it may have attacked a human. Perhaps it has been shot by a farmer while going after livestock.

A further incident could occur on 4 June.

Sixth of July could see the rise of vigilante groups, who set out to hunt the creature down.

Between 2 July and 11 August experts confirm from tracks that one of the great cats is loose. From 18 July an official, co-ordinated hunt could take place.

Around 12 August, the animal may be identified as a panther, having been trapped or shot.

SEAN CONNERY CHOOSES SCOTTISH POLITICS

L'acteur Sean Connery cesse de faire films en faveur d'une carrière à propos de la politique en Écosse. L'aigle royal est mésestimé, or il fait tôt la tumulte.

The actor Sean Connery gives up making films in favour of a career connected with Scottish politics. At first, the golden eagle is underestimated, but he creates uproar soon.

Scottish politics and the clamour for an independent Scotland feature strongly in 1994. Around 17 February, uproar breaks out in parliament and in the press.

Between 1 and 13 March, the film actor Sean Connery, after a long and acclaimed career, may be offered the opportunity of a political career in Scottish politics. He could stand for election as a Euro MP for Scotland in 1994. He has previously made party political broadcasts for the Scottish Nationalists.

If he accepts such an offer, the announcement may be made in Scotland.

Between 2 and 22 April, he could make final arrangements connected with filming, while focusing on his new career (18 April to 2 May).

During 1 to 18 May, he receives huge public and press attention, perhaps being compared to 'a golden eagle' as the symbol of Scotland's bid for independence.

The most important date is 6 June, signifying a temporary ebbing away of public interest (international events taking over at this point), but in October he may be back in the headlines with a speech around 2 October. Between 12 and 18 October he could be underestimated – but not for long.

CHANNEL TUNNEL – STRANGE EXPERIENCES

Le tunnel sous la Manche – les issues gardées parce que les voyageurs souffrent des expériences étranges. Partent de la réalité vraie, viennent d'ailleurs.

The Channel Tunnel – the exits are guarded because travellers undergo some strange experiences. They depart from true reality, they come from somewhere else.

A weird, mysterious prediction. The Channel Tunnel linking Britain and France is due to be opened in late 1993.

Between 11 February and 11 March 1994 train passengers in the tunnel apparently undergo some strange experiences, which may be hallucinatory, but believed at the time to be real. They have difficulty in convincing others that they have undergone these experiences. This difficulty may go on until 2 April.

The occurrences could receive publicity with the Channel Tunnel authorities issuing denials between 2 May and 2 May. Nevertheless, they continue to happen.

By 2 to 12 May and again on 9 June they could also become the personal experience of journalists who report them.

From 2 to 18 July the exits to each end of the tunnel may be guarded in the belief that the experiences may be caused by outside agents.

However, between 6 August and 6 to 12 September scientific investigation may come up with a solution related to the geological strata beneath the tunnel itself.

SPACE – THE DREAM OF MARS

Exploration d'éspace atmosphèrique se fourvoie. On croit qu'un voyage à la planète Mars est un rève, tandis que la réalité est près de naissance. Bol à terre!

Exploration of outer space loses its way. It is believed that a journey to the planet Mars is a dream, whereas the reality is close to birth. Fortune to the world!

Among many serious 'earthbound' predictions for 1994, this one stands out like a beacon lighting the way to humankind's destiny in the next millennium.

It begins on 2 January with a new realisation that economics are beginning to dictate the rundown of projects connected with space exploration. Budgets could be severely cut and there may also be technical setbacks.

Between 6 March and 2 May space exploration will be viewed as having lost its way, but at the end of this period there could be a stroke of luck which could, by 12 June, be seen to bring a journey to Mars much nearer. Perhaps this is a technological breakthrough.

Plans for a venture into outer space could crystallise between 11 July and 6 August.

Between 2 and 17 October worldwide attention could be focused on an exciting new space project.

AIR TRAFFIC CONTROLLERS STRIKE

La belle saison – les contrôleurs européens de la navigation aérienne se mettent en grève de la sécurité à basse altitude après une catastrophe au lycéen.

The summer months – European air traffic controllers go on strike over safety at low altitude, following a disaster at a secondary school.

Between 2 and 6 January protests among air traffic controllers may centre on low-altitude flying over populated areas – possibly a reaction to new regulations governing landing and taking off from airports.

An incident connected with the secondary school in the prediction could occur between 17 February and 17 March, the first of a series of accidents or near-misses.

Between 11 and 22 March air traffic controllers may raise problems affecting safety, not likely to be solved. Between 12 April and 12 May European controllers may band together to alter regulations affecting aeroplane altitudes.

Between 11 and 18 May controllers of several nations could strike, although it is not clear whether this includes the British. The strike could last until 2 July. Ninth of June represents a crucial point in the strike situation.

If controllers return to work at the beginning of July, some sort of catastrophe could occur around 2 August, the peak holiday period.

By 18 October regulations causing the original grievances could be altered.

BRITAIN BREAKS WITH COMMONWEALTH

Le Sécretaire du Commonwealth va, sis ailleurs de la Grande-Bretagne, tandis que les membres, nations libres, y rebellent trop contre monarque fallacieux.

The Commonwealth secretary goes, situated elsewhere from Great Britain, while the free member nations rebel to excess against the deceptive monarch.

Severance of Britain's political ties with the Commonwealth would affect a quarter of the world's population. Member nations include Canada, Australia, India, Pakistan and many African and Asian countries.

The 'deceptive monarch' could refer to Charles III, or to Britain who once directly ruled these countries. A deception occurs, or is revealed on 2 February.

During 2 to 6 March the Commonwealth secretary may publicise the response of resentful member nations.

As early as 6 to 8 April the secretariat could be located in a country other than Britain.

The source of this break may lie in Britain's links with the EC. During 2 to 5 May, nations could withdraw from the Commonwealth to form a separate association, while Britain seeks or is forced by circumstances to pursue closer political and economic ties with Europe (11 to 18 July).

Twelfth of June could mark a decisive point in this separation. By 15 August the entire Commonwealth could have opted out, leaving Britain outside the circle of nations.

From 18 October, all remaining constitutional and political links with Britain could be severed, leaving the new alliance to direct its own future.

ISRAEL – ISOLATED AMONG ENEMIES

Les gens d'Israel, une île sans secours d'Amerique, voient ses ennemis devenant plus fort. Larmes de colère à la part aux l'Égypte et les autres nations Arabes.

The people of Israel, an island lacking America's help, see their enemies becoming much stronger. Tears of rage over their portion against Egypt and the other Arab nations.

A grim view of Israel isolated among her powerful Arab neighbours, abandoned by a United States too absorbed in its own problems. Europe, too, will be occupied elsewhere.

Eleventh of January may mark some kind of low point or tragedy for Israel, or a sombre realisation among Israelis that, from now on, they will have to act alone.

After 2 February Israel may protest to America about its foreign policy, while between 11 March and 2 April the mood becomes one of anger, reflected in debate in America, but to no avail. Israel's sense of betrayal may grow stronger during the period between 6 April and 2 May, as it sees enemies arming themselves in a new association (see page 140).

Between 2 and 6 May the people of Israel feel marooned, as if on a desert island. This could be the result of a general trend, or a specific event. Around 2 July Israel may have a dispute with Egypt over borders.

From 6 to 17 September Israel will realise that she can expect no further help against her enemies.

This situation looks like it may become a grave international crisis.

NILE FAILS – EUROPE SCORNS EGYPT

*À cause de la sécheresse en Afrique le Nil devient un marais.
L'Égypte et les pays d'alentour endurent le mépris de l'Europe.
Fomente la mission barbare d'Islam.*

Because of the drought in Africa the Nile becomes
marshland. Egypt and her neighbouring countries suffer
Europe's scorn. It stirs up the barbarous mission of Islam.

For thousands of years the annual flooding of the Nile has
provided a rich source of agricultural wealth for Egypt. Now –
around 18 February – climatic change reduces the once mighty
river to marshland at a time when both America and Europe are
intensely preoccupied.

From 13 March bitterness grows. From 2 to 22 April, countries
depending on the Nile may endure the indifference of an EC
preparing to send troops into Yugoslavia for a full-scale conflict.
Egypt and other affected countries may issue an appeal, stimulat-
ing much argument, but little action.

From 1 to 2 May, Egypt and her neighbours are much stirred up
by the issue (Egypt is already much troubled by Islamic funda-
mentalist groups).

During 19 June attention will focus on Europe, while 6 August
marks a dramatic increase in the effects of widespread drought in
the African continent, to which the failure of the river Nile could
be attributed.

During 2 to 19 October Islam will receive widespread publicity.
There could be threats and terrorist attacks. This prediction is a
warning to Europe that it should not ignore what is happening in
Africa at this time.

CANNABIS LEGALISED

La Grande-Bretagne – la campagne pour la légalisation de cannabis persuade le gouvernement de traiter le stupéfiant comme un sédatif que barre troubles.

Great Britain – the campaign for the legalisation of cannabis persuades the government to treat the drug as a sedative that prevents unrest.

The 'unrest' could describe a marked rise in street crime, disturbances, and political protest. In these circumstances the legalisation of cannabis may be regarded by many as a cynical move by a government which has been so opposed to the notion.

Between 2 and 18 January cannabis could be issued to treat 'unrest' – in disturbed mental patients or difficult prisoners – against the provocative background of severe public disturbances which threaten to dislocate British society.

Between 2 and 11 February and 18 March to 18 April, private discussion by the authorities could surround the 'benefits' of calming a resentful population through the legal sale of cannabis. During 5 to 22 April, fierce public debate may erupt over the issue.

However, between 18 May and 12 June public support for such a move could increase, due to a sharp rise in violent crime and unrest during a hot summer. Legalised cannabis might also eliminate the drug culture in British prisons, now going through a turbulent period.

Between 6 and 18 July the campaign gains added momentum. Regulations permitting the use of cannabis could be introduced around 11 July.

Seventeenth of October marks a possible return to civil unrest, or the government may find itself in great difficulties with its own supporters after this decision.

TURKEY AND GREECE WAR OVER CYPRUS

Une nouvelle guerre sonne entre La Grèce et La Turquie sur Chypre blessé. La base amputé. Elle finit en le pat sot et elle fait misérable la region entière.

A new conflict rings out between Greece and Turkey over wounded Cyprus. The base cut off. It ends in a foolish stalemate and it makes the entire region destitute.

A short, bitter conflict, unhappily anticipated for a number of years, will be fought between Greece and Turkey – the cause being Cyprus, at present partitioned between both countries.

The base referred to is, perhaps, the British RAF base at Cyprus. Between 18 February and 6 March Britain may announce that the base is to be closed, despite protests by Greece, fearful that this will upset the balance of power with Turkey.

From 1 to 22 May new elements may contribute to an increasingly tense situation. Turkey may be voicing demands to occupy the whole of Cyprus.

Between 1 and 18 July war may break out, affecting the whole of the eastern Mediterranean and making it destitute for many years to come.

By 18 August Cyprus could display signs of severe damage in many areas.

Between 1 and 18 October the war could end with little or nothing gained by either side.

NUCLEAR FUSION WILL TRANSFORM EUROPE

La fusion transformera la fission de l'atome, issue de la pile couveuse, en les centrales nucléaires de la Communauté Européen. La saillie terminer époque.

Fusion will transform nuclear fission, born of the breeder reactor, in the nuclear power stations of the European Community. The 'mating' to end an epoch.

For many years, physicists have been seeking the Holy Grail of 'hot' fusion – the power that drives the sun – with technology costing millions of pounds.

The process creates helium by driving together atoms of deuterium (heavy hydrogen). Sea water contains enormous quantities of deuterium, so a successful outcome could produce almost boundless supplies of cheap energy.

But there are drawbacks. The process produces temperatures as hot as the sun's surface, together with hard gamma radiation.

A few years ago two scientists claimed to have produced controlled 'cold' fusion in a testtube with no radiation. Other scientists could not match their findings, although research is still continuing in Europe. But the worldwide interest generated by their announcement demonstrated the transforming effect on society that such a discovery would have.

This prediction indicates that the process will be discovered in 1994. It will replace nuclear fission, at present used by nuclear power stations, ending this era for ever.

The process will originate in the European Community, eventually benefiting the entire continent, east and west.

During the period between 2 and 19 February nuclear fusion emerges in Europe. The process is logical, consistent and capable of repetition – the three principles of any successful scientific experiment. An era ends with this discovery, but a new one is born. Between 17 and 19 March a decision may be taken by the European Community in connection with its nuclear power stations.

Around 18 to 22 April further decisions connected with nuclear power may be implemented.

During 2 to 23 May a controlled atomic reaction will transform the process of nuclear fission – this could relate to an important experiment or development in the process.

Between 2 and 17 October decisions concerning nuclear fusion will herald the shutdown of 'obsolete' reactors.

The importance of this prediction cannot be overestimated. Needless to say, I have decoded other predictions 'tracking' its progress after 1994 and it seems clear that this scientific discovery will transform society in just a few years and in ways that we cannot, at present, imagine.

The world will enter a new millennium equipped with a 'clean', safe energy source that imitates the power of the sun and the hydrogen bomb. Only the eyes of Nostradamus will discern how far and how fast we shall travel with such wings on our heels.

EXILE AGASSI FACES LAWSUIT

Le joueur de tennis, André Agassi, part à jamais de son foyer à Las Vegas, or un restant seul du moi ancien. D'emblée le lendemain, il est mèlé au litige que lui hait.

The tennis player, André Agassi, goes for ever from his home at Las Vegas, now only a remnant of its former self. On the following day, he is immediately dragged into a bitter lawsuit.

André Agassi, the flamboyant American tennis player, won the Wimbledon men singles title in 1992. The reference to Las Vegas being 'only a remnant of its former self' may refer to the aftermath of a great earthquake in California which Nostradamus has predicted for 1993. For many years towns and cities like Las Vegas in states surrounding California could be deeply affected.

Between 2 and 11 January Agassi's life may change for ever. He may even give up playing tennis. From 2 to 15 February he could be confused about the right course of action to pursue.

April sees him making important decisions, including leaving Las Vegas where he grew up. Having made up his mind, he may act at once to relinquish several commitments.

During the period between 26 June and 6 July he could be making headlines and life could become even more complicated when a connection with Las Vegas enters his life again on 18.

Around 19 August he could resent intrusive publicity, while from 17 to 18 October he could be dragged into a lawsuit, possibly linked with his career as a tennis player.

JULY

Electronics Teach the Deaf • Mediterranean
Beaches Become No-Go Areas • Africa – Gorillas
Under Threat • Fierce Debate Over Land •
Baldness Cured by Genetics • Genetics – The Key
to Rejuvenation • Boris Yeltsin – A Target for
Enemies • Clashes Over Scottish Independence •
Income Tax Goes Up • Genetics Reveal Ancient
Egypt • Parliament Blocks Police Bill • Market
Forces Crush Health Service • East–West
European Union • World Economy on Brink of
Collapse • Michelle Pfeiffer in British Theatre

ELECTRONICS TEACH THE DEAF

Le traitement des sourds comprend l'usage de la micro-electronique qu'offre un lien d'enseignement entre le cerveau et l'oreille. La base de départ par Basle.

The treatment of the deaf includes the use of micro-electronics that offers a teaching link between the brain and the ear. A starting point.

Micro-technology already exists to produce hearing in certain types of deafness. The hearer receives an approximation of sound range and quality.

This prediction focuses on 'teaching'. This new technology is undeveloped, so interpretation is tentative.

Eighteenth of January signals exciting new micro-electronics technology. Between 6, 18 and 23 March it could be used to make a direct link with the brain, by-passing the sensory organs altogether. Specially designed microchips could act as 'ears', receiving and transmitting signals which the brain perceives as 'sounds'.

Experiments may take place between 1 and 22 April with advances in the technology set by 2 May. Basle in Switzerland could carry out early experiments.

Alternatively, *le bas* describes a lower range of hearing than the norm, experienced by deaf people using this technology (1 to 12 May).

From 18 May, the new treatment, perhaps in the form of skin implants close to the brain, could be available.

From 2 to 18 July, the 'teaching' element comes into force. For example, it would be possible, using this technology, for profoundly deaf children to learn to speak at an early age and to attend state schools.

MEDITERRANEAN BEACHES BECOME NO-GO AREAS

Grosse pollution cotière gît sur rivages de la Méditerranée. Les dangers chimiques se dispersent aux plages puantes. Ils y barrent se balader béatement.

Heavy coastal pollution lies on the shores of the Mediterranean. Dangerous chemicals are scattered over the stinking beaches. They obstruct any blissful wandering.

Around 18 March sudden pollution may cause ecological damage on the shores of well-known Mediterranean resorts.

Alternatively, this could be the end result of a long build-up of human and chemical waste. The Mediterranean is almost entirely an inland sea, except for the narrow outlet to the Atlantic through the straits of Gibraltar. It cannot disperse waste like an ocean.

Around 6 April a major report or survey may highlight the level of pollution. Intense publicity could result (11 April to 2 May). Access to certain areas by bathers and walkers may have to be prohibited.

After 13 June chemical pollution builds up and there is a distinct bad smell. Between 6 and 13 July the pollution becomes steadily worse along the shores. Between 11 August and 6 September, dangerous, toxic chemicals could be found on the beaches.

Around 2 October, these could be dispersed in a massive effort to rid the beaches of pollution – perhaps a first step to dealing with the level of pollution in the sea itself.

Tourism is badly affected during 1994.

AFRICA – GORILLAS UNDER THREAT

Afrique – les gardiens lassés luttent contre braconniers à défendre les gorilles. Enfants et adultes tués entre végétation brulée du paradis miserable.

Africa – exhausted wardens battle against poachers to defend the gorillas. Infants and adults killed among the burning vegetation of the wretched Garden of Eden.

A sombre prediction of what will become of our cousins in Africa – the Garden of Eden where humans and gorillas evolved together. Nature reserve wardens and gorillas will be making a fight for survival against poachers, but the prospects look grim.

Around 23 February, there could be killing, possibly of poachers as they attempt to kill adult gorillas and steal their infants. During 11 March to 12 April clashes may occur between wardens defending the gorilla reserves and armed poachers.

Between 2 and 12 April the worsening situation may spur an international appeal or headline story, focusing on gorillas and infants in their natural habitat.

From 22 April to 12 May wardens could become exhausted by constantly fighting off gangs of poachers. A particularly wretched incident could occur on 15 May.

During 2 to 18 July the gorillas might no longer be defended, as their case seems hopeless. Left to fend for themselves they must survive among vegetation destroyed by fire.

In October (6 to 15) there could be a last stand, by wardens and/or families of gorillas, but the prediction may be saying that the gorilla could be lost to Africa.

FIERCE DEBATE OVER LAND

Avec tellement terre en friche un débat publique se met sur un droit de propriété. On a contesté férocement les lois d'abord. Le mal gain assaille sens moral.

With so much land lying fallow, a public debate begins over rights of property. Laws of access have been fiercely contested. The wrongful wages attack conscience.

Large tracts of land will lie fallow in Britain as a result of the EC 'set aside policy' – rewarding farmers who reduce their production. One consequence is the growing public demand for greater access to these unused areas. At present, over eighty per cent of land in Britain is owned by around ten per cent of the population.

Between 2 and 11 March access to land could be fiercely contested and even end up in the courts. In April a public debate could begin over the complex issue of rights of property. If someone owns land and they are not using it, can they deny access to others?

Between 18 April and 23 May the laws governing rights of property may come in for intense criticism and a judicial review could be set up.

The debate continues during May with much argument that conscience demands the present laws be changed because people have a moral right of access.

Around 18 August there may be a mass countrywide attempt to gain access to many areas of unused land.

The issue gains momentum in October with the focus shifting to the enormous wealth generated through the inheritance of great estates. There may be much press and public scrutiny of just who owns what, from the monarchy downwards.

BALDNESS CURED BY GENETICS

Le traitement de la calvitié embrasse une modification par la gènètique des cellules du scalp. On couvre la tête et il faut brosser, parer – or la bénéfice énorme!

The treatment of baldness includes a modification by genetics of the scalp's cells. The head is covered. It has to be brushed, dressed – now the enormous profit!

Millions of balding men all over the world (and not a few women, too) would love to have a full head of hair again. Many secret prayers may now be answered.

Between 18 February and 18 March a genetic manipulation of scalp cells containing hair follicles may be attempted for the first time on one or more volunteers.

Between 2 and 23 April, the scalp could be covered with 'fuzz' –a sure sign that the hair is starting to grow again. Growth continues during April, while during the weeks between 2 and 17 May, it is long enough to be brushed and dressed with hair preparations. By 22 May it may even have to be cut!

The important date is 18 July, signifying a public announcement or a widespread availability of the treatment.

By 2 to 13 October, other remedies for hair loss could lose public appeal, with the recognition that baldness can only be treated with complete success by genetics.

A worldly wise comment on the huge profits to be gained by such a cure completes this prediction.

GENETICS – THE KEY TO REJUVENATION

Techniques de réjeunissement embrassent globules d'air étant pompés en la peau – un acte si fou. La génétique aura la vraie réponse, transforme les muscles.

Rejuvenation techniques include globules of air being pumped into the skin – such an act of folly. Genetics will have the right answer, it transforms the muscles.

Again, we see a 'cluster' of predictions on the same theme occurring during July, this time focusing on amazing developments in genetic science.

Rejuvenation is the subject here – the centuries-old quest for the elixir of perpetual youth which may at last be within this generation's grasp.

I have not heard of the treatment, which is described so scathingly by the prediction. Perhaps it is an ironic comment, but dating suggests it could be available between 2 to 23 February and 11 May.

However, during 2 May to 17 June rejuvenation research by genetic science is rapidly moving up on these rather desperate measures. By 2 July a treatment for strengthening and rejuvenating muscle tissue, the secret of a youthful appearance, could have gone public.

By 22 August, a range of genetic techniques and new organisations will have sprung up to deal with the undoubted huge demand.

The prediction's future tense points to more exciting techniques of rejuvenation being discovered after 1994.

BORIS YELTSIN – A TARGET FOR ENEMIES

Gonflé d'orgueil, Boris Yeltsin de la république de Russie, fait beaucoup des ennemis. Assaillent le marasme, les tient basses. Mésaventure barre la trappe.

Puffed up with pride, Boris Yeltsin of the Russian republic, makes many enemies. They attack the slump keeping them down. Mishap obstructs the trap.

At the time of writing (1992) Boris Yeltsin is President of Russia. This prediction indicates that he will hold the same or an equally significant post in 1994.

Between 11 and 17 February some great misfortune, possibly economic, could befall Russia. By 5 to 12 April the country will be deeply affected by this situation, which could spread to all parts, causing deep unrest and protest.

Around 2 May, Russia could be facing an economic slump, while between 17 and 19 a trap set for Boris Yeltsin could be obstructed. This may refer to a failed political attempt to replace him, or to an assassination attempt which goes wrong.

As a result of escaping his difficulties, Yeltsin may make yet more enemies by displaying misplaced pride during 6 June and 22 July.

Between 2 and 13 October, having humiliated those who oppose him politically, he may once again face attempts on all sides to see him depart from the political scene.

CLASHES OVER SCOTTISH INDEPENDENCE

L'Écosse indépendante – la campagne rousse la scène politique.
Les Conservateurs, aspirés dans son sillage, refusent à écouter –
or barrent le tiers-arbitre.

An independent Scotland – the campaign scorches the
political scene. The Conservatives, pulled along in its
wake, refuse to listen. Now they obstruct the independent arbitrator.

Bitter political battles over independence for Scotland may be
expected in 1994.

Between 6 March and 22 April a new, or revitalised, campaign
to win independence could get under way. The campaign will
gain big headlines and from 11 March the Conservatives, possibly
alarmed by its progress, will display their total opposition to the
breakup of the United Kingdom.

Around 23 April the government will move to prevent the
campaign from acquiring political gains, but from 2 to 12 May it
may be forced to listen to the arguments. This situation could be
linked with elections to the European parliament.

The campaign may achieve an added momentum over the next
three months with the government being pulled along in its wake.
August could see 'scorching' political and public debate on the
issue.

Between 2 September and 2 October an independent arbitrator
could be appointed, by either the European Commission at
Brussels, or the European parliament, set to achieve much more
power in this year.

Around 11 September, the British government could oppose
the appointment of a foreign arbitrator on an issue relating to such
a fundamental aspect of the British constitution.

INCOME TAX GOES UP

À la Grande-Bretagne le gouvernement creuse sa propre fosse. Il est contraint d'augmenter le niveau d'impôt sur le revenu, un emblème de fiasco systematique.

In Great Britain the government digs its own grave. It is forced to raise the level of income tax, a symbol of systematic failure.

Lowering the level of income tax has been one of the main planks of government policy since the Conservatives gained power in 1979. To raise it in a year of severe recession would, indeed, be 'a symbol of systematic failure'.

The period between 2 February and 2 March is marked by the government digging even deeper into the country's financial reserves to maintain its programmes.

After 1 March to 1 April its economic policy is generally regarded as having failed and the possibility of raising income tax becomes a political issue.

However, the government may not be able to wait until the time of the November Budget, despite the opposition of many of its own backbenchers (18 March to 18 April).

Around 22 April Britain could face unexpected new expenditure which requires an increase in taxes, including income tax. This may happen between 2 and 11 May, or possibly, 6 and 18 July.

However, by 11 October the increase may not be enough and the government could once again be digging into reserves to pay for various projects.

GENETICS REVEAL ANCIENT EGYPT

Archéologie use la gènètique et la découverte criminelle aux momies d'Égypte et ses objets fabriqués. Le résultat, un pas au passé, surpasse la fable lassé.

Archaeology uses genetics and criminal detection on Egyptian mummies and their artefacts. The result, a step back into the past, surpasses the tired legend.

A third July prediction involving genetics – this time combined with forensic criminal detection to investigate bodies thousands of years old, the mummies of ancient Egypt.

Between 2 and 17 January ancient objects, or artefacts, already studied using traditional archaeological methods and thought to contain nothing more of interest, may be chosen for a fresh examination, using forensic science normally applied to the solution of crimes, including murder.

This examination could occur between 2 and 17 February. Much new information will emerge about the people who used these objects. Between 6 and 17 March these techniques may be applied to Egyptian mummies, involving the examination of skin tissue and cloth.

From 2 to 13 April, in the light of new knowledge, the mummies will appear to 'speak' to us about their lives. Between 11 May and 2 June, information flows, changing our picture of ancient Egypt beyond all recognition.

During 11 to 13 July genetic scientists may add to this knowledge. More ancient artefacts could also be examined.

Between 13 August and 17 September marks a recognition that traditional archaeology must be expanded to include these new sciences which can tell us so much about the past.

PARLIAMENT BLOCKS POLICE BILL

Le gouvernement se fait de modifier l'organisation de la police. Il rate parce que le parlement ne peut pas unir bien. On barre la tentative par suffrage du sien.

The government acts to change the organisation of the police. It fails because parliament cannot sufficiently unite. The disorganised attempt is obstructed by its own vote.

The new bill presented by the government could include the creation of a national police force, among other reforms.

Between 2 February and 18 March, it may become clear that the bill is destined for a difficult passage through parliament. From 12 to 22 April the government may be forced to modify certain key sections in the act.

Between 18 April and 18 May, strong opposition may emerge from the police, with lobbies to parliament.

During the period from 2 May to 23 June obstacles could block the progress of the bill. For instance, it could get stuck in committee stage with many amendments.

By 2 to 18 July the focus rests on the government's organisation of its own vote in the Commons, or the Lords, and the bill could complete one or two readings.

Nevertheless, from 2 to 11 October Conservative backbench opposition to the act is formidable and the bill could fall during 11 to 18.

This failure may reflect badly on the government at a time when it is experiencing acute political difficulties.

MARKET FORCES CRUSH HEALTH SERVICE

La Grande-Bretagne, le service national de santé brulé sous les rouages inlassables de l'État. Traitement des malades doit être lucratif avant l'exécuter.

In Great Britain, the National Health Service crushed beneath the unflagging wheels of state. The treatment of patients must be profitable before it is carried out.

Controversy has always surrounded the Conservative government's reforms of the health service.

During the weeks between 6 and 18 January further measures could be passed which, in the view of many, bypass the principle of free health care for all. The state seems to have become unstoppable.

Around 15 to 17 March this new programme could ensure that a patient's treatment must be seen to be profitable before it is carried out. It may be a declared policy of the reforms. Certainly, this will be the public view. Possibly the patient may also have to show proof of financial means before treatment.

During 2 to 23 April the policy may extend to serious and sudden illnesses, but the public could feel that the reforms have gone too far for protest to be effective.

In view of the severe economic situation, between 2 and 17 October the government may pursue further the idea that treatment should be profitable. Much public debate over the issue could follow.

EAST–WEST EUROPEAN UNION

L'Europe traite aux membres du Commonwealth des États Indépendants au sujet de l'union. Elle a bénéfices visibles balancés lesquels payent, bon an mal an.

Europe negotiates with the members of the Commonwealth of Independent States on the subject of union. It has visible, nicely balanced advantages which pay off, taking the good years with the bad.

This is a vision whose time will come in 1994 through compelling circumstances. With the collapse of communism, the unification of Europe will gradually be forced upon it by momentous international events.

During the week of 11 to 17 January the Commonwealth of Independent States – the countries of the old Soviet Union – may themselves broach the subject of an association with the EC, though not full membership.

From 2 to 17 March it will be recognised that full union may have distinct advantages. By 7 April an announcement could be made. Events move swiftly in the international arena (see page 00) and between 18 April and 6 May, negotiations could begin.

Around 17 August the terms of this negotiation could severely affect Britain's own relations with the Commonwealth, an association of nations which were once part of Britain's empire (see page 76).

The prediction does not mention the countries of Eastern Europe. They may be involved in a separate negotiation.

WORLD ECONOMY ON BRINK OF COLLAPSE

L'économie d'Amerique est ruiné. Japon tremble au bord d'effrondement. L'Allemagne sait bien qu'il faut se mettre seule à vaseuse Europe. Y faut faire ensemble.

America's economy is ruined. Japan trembles on the brink of collapse. Germany well knows that muddled Europe must stand alone. There, united action is necessary.

A grim prediction with lasting effects as the world economy shifts irrevocably, like a planet pulled out of its natural orbit by a maverick star. The twin pillars of America and Japan cannot stand. One is shattered and the other is fatally flawed. Germany, the only power to match them, knows that a divided Europe must unite as never before, if it is to survive and not succumb to an economic and social dark age.

Around 11 January, Japan faces severe economic depression. Repercussions follow in the world's money markets. Japan's government may introduce emergency measures.

During 2 February to 2 March Japan is torn between confused debate and the necessity to act. On 18 March we could see the country trembling on the brink of collapse. The yen could be under extreme pressure.

This threatening situation will continue from 11 April to 18 May, with the American economy in ruins from 22 April – the main cause of Japan's difficulties.

Between 13 and 17 May, the spotlight turns on Europe, the biggest potential superpower of them all, but with a centuries-old history of division. Between 17 May and 1 June the members of the EC and other nations must act decisively to prevent a total collapse of the world economy.

Eighteenth of July is a point of no return. Europe goes it alone, and on 2 October, Germany emerges as the economic dynamo of a new Europe.

MICHELLE PFEIFFER IN BRITISH THEATRE

L'acteur americain Michelle Pfeiffer habite en permanence à Londres avec sa famille. Fait une carrière heureuse en le théatre. Joue tôt les rôles en films.

The American actor Michelle Pfeiffer lives permanently in London with her family. She makes a successful career in the theatre. She soon plays parts in films.

Many American film stars are predicted to come and work in Britain during this year (see page 29). One such star is Michelle Pfeiffer.

Around 17 January she may accept an offer to work in Britain, while from 2 to 18 March she will consider moving permanently to London to further her career. This decision may become final during 18 March and 18 April.

By 2 to 23 May she could be discussing a series of offers, and around 2 to 19 June she could have one or more films lined up, or already be involved in a production.

During the days between 16 and 18 August she could make a successful début in London's West End theatre. Her name could appear in headlines around 22 August.

Between 2 and 11 October family matters could become very important to her, with a possible announcement around 7 October.

AUGUST

Eastern Europe Struggles for Tourists • A Mad
Summer Breeds Violence • World Cup Revives
America's Spirit • New Planets Spur Rethink on
Alien Life • Schools and Parents United Against
Reforms • The Blind See in Computer Graphics •
A New Plague in Africa? • Netherlands – Queen
Beatrix Abdicates • Loch Ness Monster Filmed
Underwater • Sigourney Weaver Risks Life in
California • Poverty Linked with Crime

EASTERN EUROPE STRUGGLES TO WIN TOURISTS

Hongrie, la Pologne et les autres pays d'Est, anciens régimes communistes, luttent en sablier pour l'avenir meilleur. Les sélects bècquent aux prix basses.

Hungary, Poland and the other countries of the Eastern bloc, formerly communist regimes, struggle in an hourglass for a better future. A select clientele pecks at low prices.

A plausible view of Eastern Europe during the next few years, but analysis reveals that in some countries, other than Hungary and Poland, communism may be due for a resurgence of public support. Whether it is permanent or temporary remains to be seen.

During February and March communists may win elections in seeking the eventual return of Eastern Europe to the communist fold.

Around 6 June several countries may make strenuous attempts to attract tourism as the quickest way of acquiring foreign currency.

During 1 July to 6 August, Hungary, Poland and some other countries may see the rise of monarchist movements aiming to restore former royal families. Exiled aristocrats may make determined attempts to regain estates confiscated by the communist regimes after the Second World War.

Seventeenth of September marks a low point in the fortunes of Eastern Europe, but by 2 October the situation may have begun to improve. Nevertheless, the 'struggle in an hourglass' aptly describes the daily grind of people just trying to survive, with no thought to making a profit.

A MAD SUMMER BREEDS VIOLENCE

En fol été britannique les grandes chaleurs font donner un SOS aux plusieurs gens affectés. La violence erre en les rues. Les prisons éclatent. Loi balayé.

In the insane British summer the very hot weather causes an SOS to be issued by many affected people. Violence roams the streets. The prisons erupt in anger. Law swept aside.

Summer, of course, refers to 21 June to 20 September. This prediction indicates a partial breakdown in British society accompanied by much lawlessness.

By 12 February to 2 March there may be violence and unrest in the streets. This may burst out afresh around 17 March.

During April there could be much general alarm over this situation, especially from influential and wealthy citizens who may feel themselves to be at as much risk as those in less happy circumstances.

Prison riots may explode between 1 and 2 May. By 18 May there could be tense situations between the people and the authorities with examples of lawbreaking on both sides. The government may use emergency measures to try and keep a lid on the situation.

By 2 July issues linked with civil liberties may be high on the political agenda.

Twelfth of August marks a period of high temperatures, producing an unpredictable, resentful population. Extreme weather conditions could persist into September.

Around 19 October simmering anger built up over a hot summer could spill over into many sensitive political issues.

WORLD CUP REVIVES AMERICA'S SPIRIT

La Californie, le martyr blessé tire une sébile. En l'Amerique, la coupe du monde se passe. Le faste rallume ésprit national. Le président va bénir le football.

California, a wounded martyr, takes out a begging bowl. The World Cup takes place in America. The display revives national spirit. The president goes to bless football.

The early part of the year, from 7 January to 18 April, reflects deep problems at home for the American president. Around 18 March, a major event or situation may occur as a blow to the presidency. It could affect the president's standing. America may be forced to turn to the international community for help of some kind.

Around 13 May, California will be in the news.

Between 17 May and 18 June it is agreed that the World Cup is to go ahead, despite many problems. This decision reflects the need to revive America's national spirit with spectacle and international participation.

The key date of 9 August marks the high point of this period of revival.

By 6 to 12 October, parts of America are in such difficulties that further aid from abroad is sought. The international community rushes to provide a network of supplies and resources. Between 19 and 22 November, aid begins arriving in huge quantities, reviving areas 'wounded' by a series of disasters.

References to international support for stricken regions may describe, in particular, the situation in the state of California.

NEW PLANETS SPUR RETHINK ON ALIEN LIFE

Astronomes, voyant les ciels de nuit, observent beaucoup des planètes que font le tour des étoiles. Ils ne raillent plus l'idée des gens radiodiffusant là.

Astronomers, watching the night skies, observe many planets orbiting stars. They no longer mock the idea of people broadcasting there.

In 1994 observational techniques may uncover an abundance of new planets orbiting stars, millions of light years from Earth. So many, in fact, that their very number could persuade astronomers that it is impossible for all of these planets to lack organic life. A proportion of them must also support intelligent beings.

Around 2 February the first of a series of new planets could be detected. A month later, on 1 March, the trickle turns into a flood.

During 2 and 17 April there could be much scientific debate, plus an announcement of some kind on 12 April. The idea takes hold, perhaps supported by some evidence that intelligent beings could be beaming signals from some of these planets.

Between 2 and 22 May there could be intense astronomical activity directed towards those planets which appear most likely to support intelligent life.

The key date – 13 August – could mark a new discovery.

During 1 to 17 September the belief that there are space 'people' on these planets becomes even stronger.

From 1 to 17 October there is a mood of intense frustration as it is realised that human beings have still not voyaged to other planets twenty-five years after man first stepped on to the moon. The stars mock us.

SCHOOLS AND PARENTS UNITE AGAINST REFORMS

Les écoles et lycées à la Grande-Bretagne sont unis contre les réformes du gouvernement. Les parents bombardent ces députés de lettres. Fille, fils barrés.

Primary and secondary schools in Great Britain are united against government reforms. Parents bombard their MPs with letters. Daughter and son obstructed.

The Conservative government has introduced many educational reforms – the national curriculum, periodic national tests for pupils, and opting out for schools. Further measures could be introduced before 1994.

Thirteenth of August may reflect the inability of many parents to enrol their child in the school of their choice. Moreover, it could indicate the lack of *any* school place for some children, only a few weeks before the beginning of the school year.

Earlier, during the period between 2 March and 1 April, opposition to government reforms grows stronger among secondary schools.

Between 1 and 20 April MPs could be bombarded with protesting letters from professional educators and parents.

From 1 to 16 May parents of many schoolchildren may be concerned about the limited choice of schools offered.

Around 2 to 19 July the government could be in serious difficulty and may even be taken to the European court.

This emotive issue remains prominent throughout September and many letters giving the results of appeals, or offering further information to parents, may not be sent out by the authorities until 12 October.

THE BLIND SEE IN COMPUTER GRAPHICS

Le traitement des aveugles comprend l'usage de la microélectronique. Les yeux voient en mansière semblable à realité virtuelle – à part, la naissance de vue.

The treatment of the blind includes the use of microelectronics. The eyes see in a way similar to virtual reality – in part, the birth of sight.

At first, the blind see in 'pictules', a computer-generated view of the world presented in sections, like a jigsaw puzzle in which the pieces are all squares of the same size. Micro-electronic receptors, probably skin implants on or near the scalp, may transmit electronic impulses to the area of the brain normally receiving signals from the eyes. These it interprets as images of the outside world.

Eighteenth of January marks a general breakthrough, with a special development regarding sight occurring from 18 February.

During 2 to 18 March technology produces images, followed by more developments in April. Volunteers first use it during 12 to 18 May, giving even those blind from birth a good approximation of visual reality.

During July, blind volunteers could be using this technology on a consistent basis.

By 2 October, they can live and work independently. Such a development could raise separate social implications concerning the continuation of disability payments and the elimination of a bar to employment in many areas previously closed off to the blind.

Treatment may be generally extended after 13 October.

A NEW PLAGUE IN AFRICA?

En Afrique les malades sont resserrés à une bande oblong de terre à la Somalie sans médécines ou seringues. Une maladie mysterieuse entre les baraquements.

In Africa the sick are confined to an oblong strip of land in Somalia without medicine or syringes. A mysterious illness among the shacks.

The prediction sees the emergence in the African continent of a previously unknown disease. One desperate solution may be to transport its victims to a remote area to prevent the contagion spreading.

This suggests that, firstly, a large section of territory in Somalia is uninhabited or deserted, despite intense efforts to check the famine, and, secondly, that the situation in the rest of Africa will be so difficult that this could be seen as a reasonable solution. With America and Europe engaged with their own problems, Africa could be left to fend for itself.

The mysterious disease could prove to be highly contagious, spreading through the general population during 11 January to 2 and 19 February. Transportation of the sick to Somalia could begin from 11 March to 11 April. From 2 to 19 May medicines are unavailable, although sufferers may be nursed.

At the same time – 2 to 17 May – a city of shacks may be constructed to house them.

Around 19 July, the appearance of syringes in Africa indicates the development of a vaccine to immunise the general population against the disease, but at this time there seems to be uncertain hope for a cure.

NETHERLANDS – QUEEN BEATRIX ABDICATES

Les gens des Pays-Bas focalisent sur la famille royale néerlandaise. La reine Beatrix se retire en faveur de son fils, Prince Willem-Alexander – tôt roi sûr.

The people of the Netherlands focus on the Dutch royal family. Queen Beatrix steps down in favour of her son Prince Willem-Alexander – soon, a trustworthy king.

From 12 January, discussion on the successor to Queen Beatrix may grow among the Dutch people. In 1994 she will be in her fifty-seventh year and may wish to follow the example of her mother, Queen Juliana, who also abdicated. Beatrix married a German diplomat, Claus von Amsberg, in 1966. They have three sons, Prince-Willem Alexander being the eldest.

Around 2 March, the focus of attention could be on Willem-Alexander.

During 2 to 19 April the Dutch people could be given an opportunity to express their wishes in a poll or referendum. It appears that they would like the young Prince (he will be twenty-seven) to succeed.

Between 2 and 18 May it becomes accepted that Willem-Alexander will soon be King.

During 15 to 19 August he proves himself loyal and trustworthy. He may succeed during this month, or an announcement about the succession could be made.

During 2 to 19 October excitement could grow with attention fixed on the royal family. Around 12 November, Queen Beatrix may formally abdicate.

LOCH NESS MONSTER FILMED UNDERWATER

De nombreuses personnes déclarent avoir vu le monstre de Loch Ness. Une expédition scientifique lui fait un film sous l'eau. Présente énorme bête barbare.

Scotland – numerous sightings are reported of the monster in Loch Ness. A scientific expedition makes a film of it under the water. It shows an enormous, barbaric creature.

The Loch Ness Monster may be real, after all! Over many years numerous sightings of a long-necked monster swimming in the mysterious Scottish loch have kept the legend alive, despite some well-known hoaxes. A large family of such monsters could easily exist in Loch Ness – it is twenty-four miles long and 750 feet deep in some places.

During 1 to 17 February a survey of the loch could be conducted underwater. Around 11 February, there could be a sighting, or a large object detected, which cannot be explained by the scientists with the survey.

Some members of the expedition could reveal (1 March to 1 May) that they have either seen the monster for themselves, or have reasonable evidence that it may exist.

From 6 to 7 April speculative diagrams or drawings of the monster could be shown at a press conference.

Between 1 and 19 May the shores of Loch Ness are likely to be filled with visitors, drawn there by this exciting development. Huge crowds may witness this 'enormous, barbaric creature', a beast from a bygone age, during 17 to 19 May. There may be another sighting around 11 August.

A film of the creature could be shot around 2 October. Alternatively, the film could have been made earlier in the year, but only now revealed.

During the period of 18 to 23 October the film may either prove the existence of the monster, or be exposed as a fake.

SIGOURNEY WEAVER RISKS LIFE IN CALIFORNIA

L'acteur américain à film Sigourney Weaver a du bol, étant donné qu'ayant échappé le séisme de justesse, elle risque sa vie à retourner à l'état bien des fois.

The American film actress Sigourney Weaver is lucky, given that, having missed the earthquake by a hair's breadth, she risks her life by returning very often to the state.

Oscar winner Sigourney Weaver will number one of many Hollywood stars who leave California after a period of natural catastrophe, including a huge earthquake prophesied for the state.

This prediction suggests that she will be greatly endangered at the time of the quake, only to risk her life again by returning to dangerous areas of California.

One return may occur between 2 January and 11 March 1994 when she will possibly make a documentary film about the extent of the damage.

From 6 March she may experience some kind of personal or spiritual transformation, having been so close to death, and may talk publicly about this, perhaps as a commentary to the film, or through a series of interviews during the period between 2 April and 11 May. The date 22 April signals an announcement.

During 2 to 18 May, once again leading a charmed life, she may again risk her safety in connection with California around 18 July, while escaping harm after 11 August.

From 17 October, a more optimistic, fruitful period may open up for this talented star.

POVERTY LINKED WITH CRIME

On ne peut pas faire la police. La pauvreté fixe le crime à la Grande-Bretagne. Ménace l'ossature de société. Misère a aliené les jeunes sans une lueur d'espérance.

Law and order cannot be maintained. Poverty determines crime in Great Britain. It threatens the structure of society. Destitution has alienated the young without a glimmer of hope.

Another ominous indication that the social fabric of Britain may be in danger of disintegration during 1994.

From 11 to 19 January the political issue of a social order which ignores the plight of homeless, unemployed young people may come to the fore.

Second of February marks a low point. Laws framed to deal with specific offences may be increasingly used to threaten and suppress social protest.

Crime will be an issue from 18 March to 12 April, while between 17 April and 19 May signs of a more hopeful social situation may emerge.

Between 6 May and 6 June links between poverty and crime become a political issue. From 11 June, the extent of Britain's poverty is highlighted, perhaps by a report or survey.

Around 2 July Britain could be criticised by the EC for its neglect of Britain's poor.

From 23 October, there could be an international row over this issue, as well as an alienation of the public at home.

SEPTEMBER

Jeffrey Archer – Political Dilemma ● Albanians
Flee War Zones to Italy ● Animal Activists Attack
Slaughterhouses ● British Rock Stars in Legal
Fight ● British Women head Revival ● Spain –
Bullfighting Banned ● King Charles Founds
Spiritual Retreat ● Besieged Canada Appeals to
King ● Defiant Travellers Gather Near
Stonehenge ● Tory Press Targets Major

JEFFREY ARCHER – POLITICAL DILEMMA

Il semble que l'auteur Jeffrey Archer se retire de l'axe de débat politique. On pense qu'il ne soutient le parti Conservateurs ni son ami Major. Sa langue tuée.

The author Jeffrey Archer appears to withdraw from the main focus of political debate. It is believed that he does not support the Conservative party, nor his friend Major. His tongue stilled.

From 5 to 18 January John Major may find himself in acute political difficulties. He could receive the total support of his friend, the writer Jeffrey Archer, the former MP and vice chairman of the Conservative party.

In February, Jeffrey Archer could begin to withdraw that support. Important dates are 1 to 17 February. Possibly the source of conflict is government policy.

On 18 March we could see the government making headlines, while Jeffrey Archer may continue to disagree with a policy (11 to 18 April) which will conflict with his own convictions.

During the weeks between 1 to 18 May he will be considering his political views and may at this time decide not to take part in an intense political and public debate. Difficulty arises, because he will be having to do a great deal of promotion and speech-making at this time. The period 6 to 11 July could see him resigned to being outside the world of Conservative politics, while he could be making headlines around 18 August.

During the party conference season, he makes it clear that he is no longer a friend of the party and may even make a speech to this effect around 13 October.

First of September could signify crucial political decision.

ALBANIANS FLEE WAR ZONES TO ITALY

Le peuple de l'Albanie, intercalé entre l'ancienne Yugoslavie et la Grèce, or les deux attrapés en guerres differentes, fuit en milliers sur la mer à l'Italie.

The people of Albania, sandwiched between the old Yugoslavia and Greece, now both caught up in different conflicts, flee in thousands over the sea to Italy.

Caught between two bitter conflicts, Albanians in their thousands will abandon their country to find safety via the only open route, across the Adriatic to Italy. That country will already be trying to deal with an influx of refugees from Africa.

Between 14 February and 2 March Albania grows alarmed at events in Yugoslavia. Savage fighting could occur. Equally, Albania's other neighbour Greece could face rising tension with Turkey.

Between 2 and 18 April there may be new factors in the Yugoslavian situation, while relations steadily worsen between Greece and Turkey. Around 2 May, Albanians, terrified at the possible consequences to their country, may be found trying to sail to Italy, many in unsuitable craft.

Between 2 and 18 July there will be two wars. Greece could be involved in both, since she has bitterly opposed the recognition of independence for Macedonia in Yugoslavia. She has always laid claim to that name for her northern province.

First of September may mark a sharp increase in the number of fleeing Albanians, and 1 to 18 October could see thousands arriving in Italy. By 2 to 18 November, Italy, overwhelmed by the numbers, could begin to enforce repatriation.

ANIMAL ACTIVISTS ATTACK SLAUGHTERHOUSES

Les activistes britanniques pour droits des animaux assaillent abattoirs, blessant salariés. Le public s'emballe, or le gouvernement mêlé est lent à agir.

British animal rights activists attack slaughterhouses, wounding employees. The public is carried away by anger, but the confused government is slow to act.

During 6 to 12 January there could be considerable public anger linked with the transport of live animals to slaughter. Around 5 to 12 March this fury could be translated into action by the activists recently recruited from the general public.

After 6 April they may organise and form plans in defence of the rights of animals against a confused and divided government (2 May).

Seventeenth of July could mark a publicity-seeking action, followed by government retaliation.

By 2 to 10 September plans could be set in motion to attack slaughterhouses in some way. This could happen around 2 to 3 October. Further action around 5 to 8 October could wound employees, one of them seriously. Live animal shipments to slaughterhouses may be delayed.

BRITISH ROCK STARS IN LEGAL FIGHT

La musique – le monde du rock britannique perd le flegme quand sosies des stars se mettent à graver des albums. Les labels rassemblent pour litige de barrer.

Music – the world of British rock loses its cool when look-alikes of stars begin cutting albums. Record labels get together in a legal action to stop it.

British rock stars draw huge crowds all over the world, and the British music industry is worth billions of pounds in exports. In 1994 it seems that people who *look* like rock stars, but don't necessarily sound like them, begin making albums. Style and content of records, like other forms of creative art, are subject to strict copyright, but copyright relating to a deliberate physical resemblance may have to be decided in court. I am not certain how such lookalikes could sell records, if they do not also sound like the person they resemble, but no doubt this will become clear in due course.

During 2 to 15 February these albums could cause alarm and anger in the rock world, with senior executives of record companies meeting around 1 March, perhaps to demand legislation or to prepare a test case.

An announcement will be made on 6 April, possibly relating to loss of world sales by major record stars who will by 23 April be actively seeking to prevent any further reduction.

This could happen through litigation against 'maverick' album producers around 1 to 13 July. On 13 September judgement could be given, though it is not clear in whose favour.

BRITISH WOMEN LEAD REVIVAL

Entre les gens britanniques un nouvel esprit fait une quête des résponses aux affaires grandes de la vie et la mort. C'est une spiritualité ranimant des femmes.

Among the British people a new spirit seeks out answers to the great matters of life and death. A spiritual revival led by women.

This prediction could be connected with the ordination of women priests in the Church of England. The new movement is concerned with 'great matters of life and death' – encapsulated, perhaps, in questions such as why are we here, where are we going and what do we do when we get there?

There has not been a widespread spiritual revival in this country led by women since pagan times and this is one reason why I am hesitant about categorising it as 'Christian', without further evidence. We can, however, expect it to be profound and radical, while reflecting the 'caring' ministry of women. Such a movement would fail unless many people were also raising these questions.

After 2 to 11 February the new movement gathers momentum – relating to a changed way of life by 23 March.

From 1 to 12 April looks to be confused. Interest will increase, with the movement relating to great and momentous events taking place at this time.

Around 17 May, women are making headlines. By 2 to 11 July many people, deeply disturbed by what is happening, may be starting out on a personal spiritual quest.

By 2 to 17 October the revival has added impact, while on 11 October it acquires an international aspect in becoming identified with fundamental issues between 14 and 18 October.

SPAIN – BULLFIGHTING BANNED

La course de taureaux dans l'Espagne – en fait par le gouvernement, un sujet à controverse forte sise à blessé des nations, le matador ote sa pèlerine à jamais.

The bullfight in Spain – in a government act, a subject of intense controversy located in the offence of nations, the matador takes off his cape for good.

The Spanish bullfight – a potent symbol of Spanish popular culture – has long been a source of controversy, in that ritual is used to kill an animal slowly before an audience of thousands. International debate on this issue may come to a head during 2 to 17 January, with calls to have bullfighting banned.

A spontaneous boycott by Spain's visitors could begin, while the Spanish government is sensitive to charges of public cruelty to animals at a time when it is promoting Spanish culture.

From 2 to 19 March there could be much opposition in Spain to a ban, which has its effect on the government.

During 2 to 12 April many tourists could boycott the bullfights, while strong controversy reaches fever pitch between 2 and 11 May. By 16 to 23 May the actions of other nations may force 'the matador to take off his cape'. The bullfight could be banned.

Around 6 July Spain is making headlines or breaking records as a tourist attraction once more.

After 6 October, the protection of the fierce black bulls previously reared for the bullfights comes under scrutiny.

KING CHARLES FOUNDS SPIRITUAL RETREAT

Roi Charles troisième fonde plusieurs organisations pour besoin d'établir une retraite ou personne, en vase clos, essaye de ramener le sens d'existance.

King Charles III founds several organisations for the purposes of establishing a retreat where a person, isolated from the world, can try to restore the meaning of existence.

From 12 to 19 March a public debate may occur on the spiritual value of existence closed off from the world, as in a monastic cloister. The debate will focus on the setting-up of such retreats for non-religious people who, nevertheless, benefit from experiencing an increased spiritual dimension.

Between 1 and 12 April several organisations may spring up with this aim in mind.

From 2 to 11 May these organisations could be seeking prominent patrons and King Charles, among others, may become interested.

Between 1 and 11 August, he may test some of the techniques offered on himself (these could include the latest mind-relaxation technology) and this experience could have a profound effect on him. Between 16 and 19 September, he could be tempted by the idea of longer periods in seclusion.

During 2 to 12 October such a retreat could be established with a public announcement on 6 October. He may become its patron.

This official recognition indicates that New Age techniques and philosophy could become much more widely accepted.

BESIEGED CANADA APPEALS TO KING

Le gouvernement de Canada fait un appel au roi à propos des milliers de fuyards traversant la frontière d'Amérique. Lutte à débrouiller à sens commun.

The Canadian government appeals to the king in connection with the thousands of fugitives crossing the frontier from America. It struggles to manage with common sense.

The key date of 13 September marks another point of impact for King Charles. The area of chaos is Canada. Across its border with the United States come thousands upon thousands of refugees fleeing from the effects of natural catastrophe and economic and social disorder.

From 2 to 13 January America is struggling to cope with overwhelming difficulties at home. Government and state finance will be unable to provide the scale of assistance required.

Between 11 and 18 February there may be an appeal for aid for America. The American government may oppose this, perhaps out of pride, as does the British government.

Consequently, between 2 and 18 March, tens of thousands of Americans will be crossing into Canada, where the government, during 2 to 11 April, may attempt to manage the huge influx, but could find itself appealing for aid to deal with the problem.

From 5 to 18 May Canada may act to close its borders with America, although this could prove impossible. Around 18 May, King Charles could receive a personal approach from the Canadian government to sponsor an initiative.

Around 11 June a proposal or international plan of action could be put forward. By 11 August thousands more people could be entering Canada illegally. After 18 October international action could be viewed as inevitable.

DEFIANT TRAVELLERS GATHER NEAR STONEHENGE

La communauté des voyageurs barrés rassemble en leurs milliers, non loin de Stonehenge, pour le solstice d'été. À cause de la saleté l'atmosphère se raidira.

The barred travelling community gather in their thousands, not far from Stonehenge, for the summer solstice. Because of the squalor the atmosphere will grow tense.

Stonehenge, banned from such gatherings in recent years will once more become a magnet in 1994. The prediction begins on 6 February when thousands of travellers may hold a meeting or begin to gather spontaneously. This huge encampment could last for months.

During 2 to 6 March the travelling community may feel under threat from government policy and may set up a representative council.

During 2 to 13 April there may be political protests. Without proper sanitation and other facilities the area will soon deteriorate. A tense summer is on the cards.

Around 2 May, travellers may move to a site near Stonehenge for the summer solstice on 21 June, although prohibitions preventing access to a wide area surrounding the ancient stones could be in force by 17 to 22 May. From 6 July the majority of travellers are still there.

During 2 to 15 August the atmosphere worsens. From 6 September, the travellers could lessen in number, beginning to gather again before the autumn solstice on 21 September. A long, hot summer boosts such a gathering.

A difficult confrontation or resolution could be signified for 13 September.

TORY PRESS TARGETS MAJOR

Fables tenaces seront lus en les journaux que rabaissent le premier ministre Major. Il fait saillies, mais en aparté le gouvernement est fêlé. Bref rappel.

In the newspapers persistent stories will be read that belittle Prime Minister Major. He makes witticisms, but in private the government is split. A brief curtain call.

Although the important date is 24 September, it is much earlier in the year that a deliberate 'whispering' campaign begins against John Major in a mainly Tory press – indicating that it is not likely to have come from the Left.

The campaign may originate with the right wing of the Conservative party who have grown dissatisfied with John Major's leadership. Past events suggest that this dissatisfaction could focus on his policy towards Europe. Also, the economy will not have recovered from the severe recession of the early Nineties.

'Persistent stories' surface around 11 March, lasting until 11 to 18 October, possibly damaging his authority at the annual party conference. They may attack Major as being inadequate for the job and use personal anecdote to ridicule him.

Press vilification could reach such a pitch that he is forced to respond jokingly, perhaps in a speech, on 2 October, but privately he may be losing the support of many of his fellow ministers later in the month, around 23 October.

The 'brief curtain call' relates to the month from 2 May to 2 June, indicating a personal triumph for John Major, perhaps connected with a European military operation in Yugoslavia, though it seems short-lived in view of his difficulties later in the year.

OCTOBER

Children's Rights – A Burning Issue ● Edwina
Currie – Successful Euro MP ● India and Pakistan
Stockpile Weapons ● Autumn Storms Fail to
Break Drought ● AIDS Spreads Among the
Homeless ● Domestic Computers Signal New Era
● Business Failures Triple ● The BBC – Huge
Following in Europe ● Government Blamed for
Share Price Slump ● Fury Over Drought ●
William – Prince of Wales ● China – Foreign
Television Spurs Revolution ● Prison Diet Alters
Behaviour ● Female Terrorists Strike at Irish Pact
● Saddam Hussein Menaces Israel

CHILDREN'S RIGHTS – A BURNING ISSUE

Droits des enfants deviennent issue brulante. Se met au barrage – par milliers parents protestent auprès des politiciens britanniques. Marée l'étouffe.

Children's rights become a burning issue. It begins a barrage – parents in their thousands protest to British politicians. The rising tide quenches it.

Children are beginning to acquire legal rights of their own. For example, the Children's Act of 1989 permits children to apply to the courts for permission to live with the people of their choice, which need not include either parent. By 1994 legislating for many more rights is being hotly debated, at least in Britain. This controversy may come about from regulations originating in the EC.

Around 2 February there could be a barrage of such regulations being passed.

By 2 to 22 April the implications of such laws will have begun to make an impact. Many parents may feel that they have lost the right to bring up their children as they see fit. Consequently, the public debate will be heated.

During 11 to 23 June the argument will sway back and forth.

Around 1 to 2 October British politicians may move to prohibit this legislation from being enacted in Britain. However, thousands of parents who are in agreement with the new legislation could then be up in arms and protesting vehemently to MPs (2 to 11 October).

Around 11 to 12 October, the issue, instead of being resolved, will now be near the top of the political agenda, destined to trouble the government for some time to come.

EDWINA CURRIE – SUCCESSFUL EURO MP

Edwina Currie, or un député fort en le parlement européen, possède une manière satisfaite. Là, elle est réceptive aux gens basses en lamentables affaires.

Edwina Currie, now a formidable member of the European parliament, possesses a pleasing style. She is receptive to the poorest people in deplorable circumstances.

One of the new MPs elected to the European parliament in 1994 will be Edwina Currie, who will begin a successful career there.

Between 2 and 11, and 23 February, she could be concerned with European matters and the forthcoming election.

Around 11 March she will be making headlines. Between 2 and 11 April she will be making speeches and will be about to become a formidable presence on the European scene, possibly talking a great deal about the plight of the poor in Europe and those left destitute and homeless by the conflict in Yugoslavia.

From 2 to 18 May she could be visiting shelters and aid centres for the poor, while at the same time doing much to draw attention to their circumstances.

Between 11 and 12 June she is becoming a familiar figure in European affairs and may at this time be working very hard to learn about European matters.

By 2 October, she could have a recognised 'political style' which gets things done.

INDIA AND PAKISTAN STOCKPILE WEAPONS

*Les deux pays l'Inde et le Pakistan, anciens ennemis, se mettent
à reserver les armes que peuvent user plus tard. Dans
l'intervalle, la foi goguenarde falsifiée.*

Both the countries India and Pakistan, former enemies,
begin to stockpile weapons for later use. In the mean-
time, the mocking faith falsified.

India and Pakistan have often been troubled neighbours since
partition of this huge territory by Britain, during the granting of
independence in 1947. India is the home of Hinduism, though
with a large Muslim population, while Pakistan is a leading
Islamic nation.

Between 2 and 11 March there could be a cessation of the
dispute between the two countries, which, far from improving
the situation, may give time to both to consider what they would
do in the event of later conflict.

During the period of 2 to 6 April tension between them grows
again. From 2 to 17 April India may be making a series of
announcements concerning the two countries.

Between 2 and 11 May one or both countries could begin to
stockpile arms for a possible conflict.

Around 12 June the rate of stockpiling could accelerate sharply,
and 17 July could be marked by unhelpful comments from one
side about the religious faith of the other.

From 17 to 26 October a deception could be practised or come to
light, while Pakistan could be looking back to India as it was
before partition in 1947.

AUTUMN STORMS FAIL TO BREAK DROUGHT

Aux derniers trois mois de l'an, le temps est lunatique, avec grandes tempètes ronflantes, mais peu pluie. La sècheresse limitée continue. Raser les barrages.

In the last three months of the year, the weather is temperamental, with great roaring storms, but no rain. The restrictive drought continues. It will raze the dams.

Autumn refers to the period between 21 September and 20 December.

Eleventh of October may signify the beginning of the season of violent electrical storms described in the prediction. A further important date could be 19 November.

But the build-up to this situation begins much earlier in the year, with at least one major storm, possibly occurring as early as 2 to 3 April.

By 20 to 25 June Britain is in the grip of a serious drought. Little or no rain will fall during the summer months, with a visible effect on the country's water resources by 8 July. Dams and reservoir structures may possibly show deterioration and cracks by 1 to 3 September.

Between 2 and 6 October, weather patterns over Britain could become very erratic. This situation may last to the end of the year, with a series of tempests which do nothing to break the drought's stranglehold.

AIDS SPREADS AMONG HOMELESS

À la Grande-Bretagne on trouve la maladie SIDA à la faveur de la nuit entre ceux feutrés qui sont sans foyer – y propage autour de feu sous les arches des ponts.

In Great Britain the disease AIDS is to be found under cover of darkness among the muffled, homeless people – here it spreads around fire under the arches of bridges.

AIDS is visualised as a deadly, creeping mist spreading among the 'muffled' people – the silent underclass, without help and hope, except for what they find on the streets.

The HIV virus is transmitted mainly through unprotected sex and the exchange of syringe needles for taking drugs. Destitutes cannot afford condoms, and so, afraid of drawing attention to drug habits that could bring down the law, they are unprotected from AIDS.

During 2 to 19 January evidence could emerge on how rapidly AIDS is spreading among the homeless, perhaps officially denied on 11. Between 2 and 13 February the media may highlight the issue after spending time with the 'night people'. During 12 to 18 March more evidence becomes clear on HIV's rate of transmission.

Between 2 and 18 April there could be a European focus on the spread of AIDS among the British homeless.

Following a European directive homeless people must be housed, and an operation begins betwen 2 and 17 May to notify those entitled to this right.

Around 12 July, British preventative measures to stop the virus spreading may not be considered adequate. From 2 August, there could be another 'sweep' of the places where homeless people go, in an attempt to bring them into proper housing and medical care.

DOMESTIC COMPUTERS SIGNAL NEW ERA

Les ordinateurs des gens ressemblent aux calculettes, mais ils tiennent le pouvoir d'absorber bibliothèque d'information parée. L'ère fade se met à aller.

Domestic computers resemble pocket calculators, but they hold the power to absorb a library of prepared information. The dull era begins to disappear.

Powerful computers resembling pocket calculators may make their first appearance around 11 March.

From 2 to 18 April they have an impact on the domestic market. One hand-held computer has access to a whole library of information. Until now computers have been confined to an élite able to understand the 'jargon'. These new computers will command mass-market appeal – people will use them as they use TV sets, videos and camcorders.

The new technology troubles the authorities. From 1 to 23 May information can be accessed by the general public in a way never known before. Previously, such knowledge has always been 'channelled' by government and other authorities – films are categorised, broadcasting is licensed by the government and there is only so much information you can get from a book.

With computerised information networks, control by the establishment will be seen as breaking down (1 May to 23 May).

Between 2 August and 1 October the system makes available an array of knowledge with which people inform themselves about issues of concern.

On 6 October there could be an official announcement voicing anxiety, but coming too late to restrict this development.

BUSINESS FAILURES TRIPLE

L'économie de la Grande-Bretagne – au lieu d'un semis, un fossé où poussent mauvaises herbes. Triples les affaires ferment. Le pays sans emploi. Barrière tient.

The British economy – instead of a seed bed, a ditch where weeds grow. Business shutdowns are tripled. The country without work. The barrier holds.

A bleak picture emerges of Britain's economy throughout 1994. The period between 11 and 22 February will be marked by a rising tide of bad debt. Many small companies – the seed bed of the future – will go under.

Between 11 and 18 April the state of the British economy may become a subject of debate in the EC. It is certainly the top issue in the UK.

During 1 and 2 May the amount of unemployment will be causing great concern. There may be a wide-ranging initiative to get the unemployed to carry out environmental work in the community. By 2 June, the rate of business failure has tripled and a corresponding rise in unemployment is likely.

Around 17 July the EC could again be discussing Britain's economy, or Britain could be making headlines across Europe and the world.

By 11 August the business environment will have become stagnant, and between 2 and 19 September the cutting-back of Britain's business base will be causing real concern for the future. The rate of insolvency continues unchecked, perhaps confirmed by figures emerging around 16 October.

Increasingly fierce demands emerge for wholesale reforms in the constitution and government of Britain, now seen as barriers to growth. Many people will believe that only then will Britain's fortunes be revived.

THE BBC – HUGE FOLLOWING IN EUROPE

Émissions par un satellite de la BBC fleurent en l'Europe plus large. On selectionne les mêmes programmes, mais suivant la langue. Bât les auditeurs loyaux.

BBC broadcasting by satellite flourishes in the wider Europe. The same programmes are selected, but according to language. It builds up a loyal audience.

Viewers in different countries who watch these satellite broadcasts will have access to a decoding device. When programmed with the correct code, the device offers a translation of what is being said in the viewer's own language. Millions of people across Europe could therefore watch these programmes together.

The first signs of such a build-up of devoted followers occur between 2 and 17 February.

Second of March could see the complex and huge operation of supplying the language decoding devices in full flow.

By 2 to 5 April the European audience for BBC programmes is rapidly increasing and around 17 May audience viewing figures across Europe for some of these programmes could be charted for the first time.

At first, not all languages can be catered for, but around 17 to 19 July, the number of available languages is significantly extended.

At first the number of multiple-language broadcasts could be limited, but around 6 October their number may increase, with more added after 5 November and the promise of many more to come after 2 December.

GOVERNMENT BLAMED FOR SHARE PRICE SLUMP

Londres rejette tôt la responsabilité de prix des valeurs mobilières au marché financier, au plus bas, sur une faillite de la politique du gouvernement.

London soon places the responsibility for the price of shares on the stock market, at rock bottom, on the failure of government policy.

Around 13 January there could be a public dispute between the government and the City of London over the handling of the economy.

From 2 to 23 February the financial market may see a rapid descent in the price of shares – a hot issue during 11 to 12 March.

Between 1 and 18 April there is a period of much confusion and argument focusing on the London share market.

During 6 to 17 May the government may announce measures which will affect shares and the stock market from 1 June to 5 August. Accusations may be levelled that politics are interfering in the free actions of the money markets.

Between 2 and 18 October the price of shares could fall precipitately, with arguments about who takes the blame.

FURY OVER DROUGHT

Pluie brève à Grande-Bretagne. De toutes parts furie envers les autorités qui contrôllent les rivières. À sècheresse, lois à assainir l'eau seront balayer.

Little rain for Great Britain. From all sides fury towards the authorities controlling the rivers. With the drought, laws on purifying water will be swept away.

The key date of 13 October indicates heightened awareness that restrictions on the use of water will be imposed throughout the winter of 1994 to 1995.

Numerous dates show a gradual build-up to a hostile atmosphere, with little rainfall in Britain between 6 April and 12 October, the latter indicating serious warnings, or emergency measures. Southern Britain has suffered most from the drought, but 'from all sides' hints that the North will also become affected, public debate occurring from 5 April to 12 May and on 6 August.

Public 'fury' towards the river authorities may erupt, as consequences of actions taken become apparent, over the profligate use or pollution of precious river water by industry, while domestic consumers are severely restricted.

Britain could be suffering severe drought by 12 August, with standpipes in the streets and the prospect of disease from water pollution.

Earlier, between 2 February and 2 May, proposals may emerge to relax regulations governing water purification in order to maintain the supply. Between 13 May and 13 October such action may be implemented, with the tacit consent of the government.

By 6 August, a serious situation could result in regulations being ignored in the race to supply water.

WILLIAM – PRINCE OF WALES

William, premier fils de Charles et Diana, devient Prince de Wales. Voue à obeir le roi, son père, mais sa mère sage, or femme de mythe, est quasi dessus les gens.

William, elder son of Charles and Diana, becomes Prince of Wales. He vows to obey the King, his father, but his wise mother, now a woman of legend, almost rules the people.

Thirteenth of October seems late for Prince William to be invested as Prince of Wales at Caernarvon Castle – his father took part in the ceremony in July 1969. He is also young, only twelve years old in 1994.

Nevertheless, he takes vows, so this may presage more than a simple announcement that he is to become Prince of Wales. Intense interest will focus on William as Britain's next king.

From 17 February the 'cult' of Queen Diana threatens to overshadow the monarchy. Between 11 and 19 March William may learn of his elevation and news could be leaked during the period of 1 to 6 April, with Diana and William receiving huge press attention. During 1 to 19 May the King could formally announce that Prince William is to become Prince of Wales.

Around 13 July a wise decision may be taken.

During 2 to 6 August the King will again have to contend with the public image of the Queen, now almost a legend. From 19 September the people could learn that Prince William is to be ceremoniously invested in what many will regard as a mini-coronation. This could happen in October, at which point William, though remaining the son of the King, may be regarded as the premier royal figure in the monarchy – a symbol of the new millennium.

CHINA – FOREIGN TELEVISION SPURS REVOLUTION

On galvanisera le peuple Chinois quand un réseau télévision se met à faire les émissions étrangers. Ils se rassemblent en lutte à liberté de faire partis.

The Chinese people will be galvanised when a national television network begins broadcasting foreign programmes. They gather together in a struggle for freedom to form political parties.

This prediction could be linked with another stating that the BBC will gain a huge following across Europe with satellite broadcasts. Many Chinese will possess the technology to receive these transmissions from 11 March.

Between 2 and 23 April the broadcasts may be involved in a struggle to install democratic freedom. China is currently going through an economic revolution, adopting free-market principles, while retaining a communist system.

After the important date, 6 April, a network could form during 2 to 6 May, connected with the viewing of these programmes and also the exchange of information.

Between 11 July and 22 August links may be formed between Chinese people and foreigners. Alternatively, the Chinese government may introduce measures to prevent free exchange of ideas between the Chinese and foreigners.

Around 2 to 12 September an organisation with political aims could be formed. The people could take to the streets.

During 2 to 17 October broadcasts could spur demands for democratic freedoms, galvanising the Chinese people to seek the end of a restrictive political system.

PRISON DIET ALTERS BEHAVIOUR

Les liens systématiques sont établis entre la nourriture et le crime. Aux prisons on introduit un régime sévère que modifie rapidement l'ambiance à l'une de la paix.

Systematic links are established between food and crime. A strict diet is introduced in the prisons that rapidly changes the atmosphere into one of peace.

Between 2 and 17 February many disturbances could take place on the streets, with other evidence of a widespread breakdown in law and order. By 1 to 6 March the habitual lawbreaker could become the subject of public debate.

During 1 to 17 April evidence of how quickly people revert to peaceful behaviour after a change in diet forms the basis of such an experiment in Britain's prisons. Similar tests have already taken place in some American states, as well as schemes in Britain involving the calming of hyperactive children.

During the period of 2 to 11 May a pilot scheme could show that prisoners do benefit from a strict dietary regime. Around 23 July measures could be put forward to extend the scheme to all or many prisons.

During October, reports emerge of a markedly more peaceful atmosphere in Britain's prisons after the introduction of this diet, probably during 2 to 11. It is confirmed that diet influences attitude and behaviour.

After 18 October changes in the way prisons are run could promote a less repressive atmosphere.

FEMALE TERRORISTS STRIKE AT IRISH PACT

L'IRA joue son va-tout d'empêcher un pacte sur L'Irlande du Nord entre La Grande-Bretagne et La République d'Irlande fait à Bruxelles. Le terrorisme à femmes.

The IRA risks all to prevent an agreement on Northern Ireland between Great Britain and the Republic of Ireland made at Brussels. Terrorism by women.

From 13 January a concerted attempt by the European Community begins to settle the problem of Northern Ireland.

Negotiations could take place at Brussels with the government of the Irish Republic. Consequently, the details of an agreement could emerge around 18 March.

Further negotiations could take place between 6 and 23 April involving Great Britain, the Irish Republic and representatives of the Northern Ireland community.

From 18 May the IRA may formulate plans to prevent such an agreement being ratified, although a pact could be in place around 2 July.

Around 2 August the IRA could attempt to disrupt this agreement with an act of terrorism, using female agents to arouse less suspicion. As a result, emergency measures could be taken by Brussels against the IRA on 18 August.

The key date of 18 October could mark the signing of the political agreement at Brussels. This prediction demonstrates the increasing power of the European Community over British affairs.

SADDAM HUSSEIN MENACES ISRAEL

Saddam Hussein d'Iraq focalise sur une ligue nouvelle des pays Arabes. L'intention est élimination rapide d'Israel. Le belliqueux resserre le rond de la peur.

Saddam Hussein of Iraq focuses on a new league of Arab countries. The aim is the rapid elimination of Israel. The warmonger draws tight the ring of fear.

A prediction signifying the beginning of a grim train of events.

During the period between 2 and 12 February proposals for a new league of Arab nations, including Iraq, will cause great alarm in Israel, particularly from 19 February.

Between 1 and 17 April Saddam Hussein, the leader of Iraq, may make several announcements, urging the rapid formation of such an alliance.

The association could be formed by 19 May.

Between 6 July and 6 August Saddam Hussein and Iraq will be the focus of world attention.

Around 1 to 2 October moves to encircle and restrict Israel could begin, with the new Arab league focusing more and more on the ambition of ending the future of Israel as a Middle Eastern state.

NOVEMBER

Princess Anne Rivals Queen Diana ● Physics
Theory Leads to Space Travel ● David Owen –
Social Democracy Revived? ● Bestsellers – Female
Heroes Top Charts ● Genetics Scientists
Prosecuted ● Anglican Church – Talks with Islam
● Gurkhas Heroic in Yugoslavia ● World Fame
for Actor Robert Lindsay ● British Reject Space
Station ● Science Computes New Technologies ●
Are People Only Computer Images? ● British
Commandeer Yugoslav Hotels ● Thatcher Quits
House of Lords ● Victoria Wood – TV Series

PRINCESS ANNE RIVALS QUEEN DIANA

À la Grande-Bretagne Anne, la Princesse Royale sage dure fols essais de la mettre sur un piédestal à l'ombre d'une monarchie que vive par la reine seule, Diana.

In Great Britain Anne, the wise Princess Royal, endures fantastic attempts to put her on a pedestal in the shadow of a monarchy that lives through Queen Diana alone.

During 2 to 19 January the charity work of the Princess Royal could be compared with that carried out by Queen Diana. Around 11 February a book, or a series of articles, could focus on the life and work of Princess Anne.

During 6 to 19 March Princess Anne may be overshadowed by publicity surrounding Queen Diana. Between 2 and 19 April efforts could be made to concentrate public attention on Princess Anne and her importance to Britain, but during 18 to 19 attention returns as always to Diana. This to-ing and fro-ing may represent alarm in some quarters that the monarchy is becoming too much identified with the Diana 'cult' which began in the 1980s.

Around 2 May, the focus concentrates on Diana alone, but events may cast a shadow on 19.

During 18 to 22 June, Princess Anne may come in for special praise and receive much acclaim from abroad for her work. On 18 August the British monarchy is making headlines.

From 11 October there could be fantastic attempts to promote Princess Anne as a rival to the Queen.

PHYSICS THEORY LEADS TO SPACE TRAVEL

Une découverte à la physique se met à faire sur ensemble en penser au sujet de l'univers. La théorie renferme un lubrifiant aux pièces. Là tôt, le sas spatial.

A discovery in physics begins to create unity in thinking about the universe. The theory contains a lubricant for the parts. Then soon, the airlock to space.

A physics discovery gives rise to a theory which eventually leads to a new form of space travel. The technology is as yet unknown.

From 2 January the physical universe may be the subject of scientific and public debate.

Between 2 and 18 February answers may emerge to certain questions. This leads on to a unifying theory which could explain much that is still a mystery about how the different parts of the universe work and act together.

The period 2 to 11 March focuses on different aspects of the universe viewed in the light of this theory.

During 6 to 11 April a scientific discovery could be made, and between 11 and 17 May excitement could grow, as it is realised that this discovery could herald a new approach to space travel.

Around 12 June a period of intense thought could produce a further exciting theory.

From 11 to 17 October, first moves in the planning of an important space project could occur, with a special announcement on 14.

DAVID OWEN – SOCIAL DEMOCRACY REVIVED?

Le Démocrat Social David Owen, de la noblesse, vu glissement electoral à ses politiques, impart ses espoirs au rassemblement qu'y parle de rentrer l'arène.

The Social Democrat David Owen, among the Lords, seeing the electoral swing to his policies, pins his hopes on the assembly that discusses re-entering the arena.

David Owen was Labour's foreign secretary in the 1970s. As one of the 'Gang of Four' he co-founded and then led the Social Democratic party during the Eighties. Following the merger of his party with the Liberal Democrats, he took his seat in the House of Lords in 1992. In the same year he became co-chairman (with Cyrus Vance) of the Yugoslavian Peace Conference, overseeing the seemingly hopeless task of bringing the complex civil war there to an end.

From 13 February 1994 David Owen may perceive signs that social democracy could once again have a future in Britain. Between 2 and 17 March further evidence emerges of a swing in public support to social democratic policies.

Between 1 and 18 April he could be in the spotlight with publicity and speeches. From 2 to 22 May he may be torn between remaining in the Lords and returning to the Commons.

Around 2 June he could make an announcement, and by 2 July plans could be set in hand for a conference to decide on the reforming of the Social Democracy party. This could take place around 11 to 13 September.

By 2 October there could be a further groundswell of public support. This prediction may herald a re-alignment on the Right of British politics.

BESTSELLERS – FEMALE HEROES TOP CHARTS

De romans populaires bradés à mysteres ont histoires des personnalités féminins de vaillance, enjambant les obstacles fabuleuses. Le bébé, un autre thème.

Popular cut-price mystery novels have stories about courageous female characters striding over incredible obstacles. The baby, another theme.

A prediction for a publisher's diary! Around 16 January to 17 March books come on to the market about women facing incredible odds. Between 6 and 17 April many books are being offered at low prices, perhaps signifying the end of the Net Book Agreement between publisher and bookseller, which standardises book prices.

'The baby' is another selling theme, but not in the familiar mother and baby-care style. Predictions show that, biologically, we will be discovering much about children and adults. Books may reflect this new knowledge.

During 17 to 22 May, women, both as fictional characters and writers, will be popular. Beginning 11 to 17 August, the height of the holiday trade, the book-buying public may turn in large numbers to books which tell a good story.

From 2 to 6 September there could be a popular vogue for novels with a fantastic mystery at their heart. Eleventh October may see a series of books being published about courage in various forms.

These themes reflect changing public tastes in a time of severe depression and uncertainty.

GENETICS SCIENTISTS PROSECUTED

En la biologie le flux de savoir génétique resserre parce que la résistance s'élargira. On applique les statuts contre tenants myriades. Bref, mole barre.

In biology the flow of genetic knowledge narrows because resistance will widen. Laws are enforced against myriad defenders. Briefly, the breakwater, the harbour boom, dams up.

New knowledge about our capacity to change ourselves and the world around us always has the power to disturb. Because of just such alarm, genetics scientists may be prosecuted in a futile attempt to prevent experimentation – futile, because any suppression can only be temporary. Knowledge will win out.

Around 11 to 12 March resistance to work involving genetic science will grow. Scientists will defend what they do. Around 2 April discoveries occur. Their implications cause even more alarm.

Between 2 and 13 May a barrier goes up and scientists may find themselves prohibited from carrying on research.

Nevertheless, such knowledge will spread and increase between May and July. Laws could be applied to prevent its spread and also to prosecute scientists. Calls could be made for all genetic research to be halted.

During the period of 2 to 18 August certain restrictions could be lifted. Alternatively, the flow of research could narrow to a trickle under new laws.

During 2 to 6 October, the impossibility of stopping the spread of knowledge may be realised. So numerous are the biological discoveries being made at this time that legislation proves powerless.

ANGLICAN CHURCH – TALKS WITH ISLAM

L'église d'Angleterre lassé, où les baptèmes en fonts se rabaissent fait un simulacre d'ensemble moral. L'archéveque de Canterbury tient des propos à l'Islam.

The exhausted Church of England, where Christenings in the fonts are reduced, makes a pretence of moral unity. The Archbishop of Canterbury holds discussions with Islam.

The Church of England has been through a series of long, drawn-out internal battles lately, most notably on the ordination of women priests. This year will see a reduction in the baptism of infants, perhaps partly as a protest by those Anglicans who object to this new development.

The Archbishop could be holding talks with Muslim leaders in Britain, or, possibly, in connection with Middle Eastern problems boiling up at this time.

The period 2 to 6 March sees the Archbishop being the strong man of the Church, holding it together in the midst of crisis.

During 2 to 11 April there could be much confused debate about where the moral unity of the Church now lies.

From 17 to 22 the Church could see a proposal for groups of Anglicans to resign from the Church, which could be close to schism.

Beginning 13 July the number of infants being baptised into the Church could be sharply reduced. Church and country could be exhausted by the force of argument.

Between 11 August and 17 September the Archbishop may be making plans to hold important discussions with Muslim leaders.

WORLD FAME FOR ACTOR ROBERT LINDSAY

L'acteur Robert Lindsay tient un rôle lassé en télévision drame, peut-être à propos d'un Slav bas, farfelu, rabourgri, que le fait célèbre dans le monde entier.

The actor Robert Lindsay takes on an exhausting part in a television drama, perhaps in connection with a mean-minded, eccentric and stunted Slav, that makes him famous throughout the world.

Robert Lindsay's career has included TV's *Citizen Smith*, success in London and New York in the musical *Me and My Girl* and the psychologically wounded Michael Murray in Channel Four's political drama *GBH*; he has also pursued a distinguished career on the stage. One of his latest stage parts is Cyrano de Bergerac.

His new role is described in precise terms. Significantly, this fame will come through television which will be even more powerful internationally from 1994.

The interpretation is tentative, but it seems that the 'mean-minded Slav' character acquires an independent fame during 11 February to 18 March, perhaps in a book, play or film script.

By 2 April Robert Lindsay could be brought into discussions. Creating a character who possesses marked physical and emotional defects (not to mention the accent!) will demand a tiring commitment. Also, Lindsay may have just played a character or a series of characters just as exhausting. Health could be a factor.

During 2 to 18 May he could be offered the role and begin filming from 18 August. An international broadcast could go out as early as 1 to 22 October.

BRITISH REJECT SPACE STATION

Dedans Europe un plan sérieux croit à propos d'une station fait dans l'éspace. C'est le premier pas à la base sur la lune. Le gouvernement britannique le refuse.

Within Europe a serious plan grows in connection with a fully developed space station. It is the first step to a base on the moon. The British government rejects it.

Far from being a single project, the proposed space complex is only the first step in a serious plan to put a base on the moon. The project originates from the EC, otherwise Britain would have no part to play in it. Economic considerations could be the motive for her refusal to take part.

Around 18 January, a moon-base project could be proposed. One wonders why, in such a difficult world economic situation, this notion flourishes – where would the money come from?

Perhaps the project is stimulated by the fact that 1994 will mark the twenty-fifth anniversary of the first landing on the moon. Public and politicians alike realise that until we have established a base there, we will not have progressed beyond that first landing.

The discovery of numerous planets in other star systems may make it more likely that other space peoples have also established themselves on satellites. The thinking could be 'if they've done it, so can we!'

Safety could well be a third factor. Concern could be linked with the number of times in its past that Earth has been hit by large meteorites and even asteroids. The moon's surface, devoid of atmosphere and vegetation, is pitted with scars from these impacts.

One theory gaining ground about the death of the dinosaurs sixty-five million years ago is that just such a huge chunk of rock came whirling out of space to crash on the Earth's surface with tremendous force and speed. Its impact darkened Earth's skies, cooled the temperature and set in motion a complex environmental chain of events that led to the extinction of two-thirds of all species, including the dinosaurs. One of those that survived was a small ratlike creature – the ancestor of humans.

The same thing could happen again – only this time humans are the dominant species and the technology which dinosaurs never possessed could save us.

By 1994 the evidence piling up for these destructive impacts in our past could raise serious questions as to how often it is likely to happen in the future. The moon-base could be proposed as a watchtower for asteroids heading towards the planet. Foreknowledge means that we might be able to destroy them before they destroy us.

But before the moon-base, there must be a space station.

Whatever the reason for the proposal – survival, or a renewed eagerness to explore space – the plan to put a base on the moon is active by 2 to 19 February. At this point, the British government refuses to take part.

Nevertheless, discussion grows during 5 to 11 March and by 2 to 11 April a serious and detailed plan has emerged. This is a project which will be wholly funded and operated within Europe (though it is possible that, because of the predicted situation in America, many American space scientists could now be working in Europe). Around 6 April an announcement could be made.

Between 6 and 12 May, attention could be focused on plans for a space station as an interim base between Earth and the moon.

During 2 to 18 June this entire project could be regarded as just the first step in a prolonged space exploration lasting into the next millennium. This realisation is linked with the discovery of a process producing nuclear fusion, also predicted for June. Such a discovery would ensure boundless, cheap supplies of energy and no doubt have a profound effect on the costs of sending rockets into space.

By 19 October, plans could be fully developed and the construction may begin.

Knowing as I do what is predicted for later years I cannot emphasise too much the importance of this prophesy – it signifies the beginning of a profound train of events stretching far into humanity's future.

GURKHAS HEROIC IN YUGOSLAVIA

Les soldats de Népal font une partie de l'armée britannique envoyé à l'ancienne Yugoslavie. Leur combat mobilisable dépasse bien ses nombres – as sur terre.

Nepalese soldiers form part of the British army despatched to the old Yugoslavia. Their fighting strength far outweighs their numbers – an ace on the ground.

The important date of 11 November indicates that fighting is still going on in Yugoslavia later on in the year, following the intervention of a massive joint European force in the early summer.

During 11 to 18 March British troops could be sent to areas of Yugoslavia, in preparation for a larger, main force.

Between 2 and 22 April considerable British forces will be despatched to Yugoslavia. Part of this force will consist of Gurkha troops, a fraction of the total number.

During 6 to 19 May these fierce soldiers from the hills of Nepal become renowned for their bravery and ability to influence the outcome of a battle – 'an ace on the ground'. Their courage is already legendary to the British people, so this new fame could arise in Europe.

By 11 to 17 October they have made a significant contribution towards the pacification of the former Yugoslavia.

During November, their courage could be highlighted.

SCIENCE COMPUTES NEW TECHNOLOGIES

Les ordinateurs – développements comprennent se ramifier en plusieurs autres sciences telle que la biologie. Forment tôt la base à myriade des bels arts.

Computers – developments include branching out into other sciences such as biology. Soon they create the foundation of myriad beautiful arts.

Computers are going to take several giant leaps forward in the next few years, linking up in unimaginable ways with other sciences, particularly biology. This 'merging' will produce entirely new techno-sciences, so subtle and flexible in their application that they can be compared to humanising arts, rather than sciences, viewed as rather 'cold' by many outside the profession.

During 2 to 11 March a definite possibility exists that a whole range of sciences could link up with computing technology in a completely new way. Between 1 and 22 April a programme could be activated and an announcement could be made around 6.

During 2 and 13 May the emphasis switches to biology, where the application of new technology forms the basis of much new adaptable and subtle knowledge. Evidence of the possibility of these 'beautiful arts' emerges around 17.

From 11 June several major developments in this field could be happening. Between 1 and 11 October events happen thick and fast, with possibilities of new technologies opening up in many other branches of science.

Eleventh of November reflects growing interest in these technologies as they develop practical uses.

ARE PEOPLE ONLY COMPUTER IMAGES?

L'étude du système nerveux des humains révèle une ressemb-
lance frappante avec système d'ordinateur. Ébranle foi – les gens
sont rien de plus qu'images d'art.

Study of the human nervous system reveals a striking
similarity to a computer system. It shakes faith – people
are nothing more than skilful images.

Clearly, this statement is related to the previous prediction.

Modern biological and genetic techniques are beginning to
reveal the basic principles upon which the human body is
constructed. Such techniques arouse not only wonder, but also a
range of disturbing questions.

The human nervous system is discovered to be strikingly
similar in many ways to the workings of a modern computer.

Religious faith is shaken by the realisation that all the activity
within our bodies and brains, the way we speak, act and think,
can be compared to ingeniously designed 'images' on a 'screen',
playing out pre-programmed commands. Many others, not
religious, but believing in humanity's independence and
creativity, may also experience doubt.

During 1 to 17 February research could reveal similarities
between the workings of the nervous system and the way a
computer, once programmed, can act independently of its
operator. More revelations follow between 11 and 19 March.

Between 1 and 17 April a convincing argument emerges that the
nervous system is nothing more than an extremely powerful and
ingenious computer.

During 2 to 11 May much of this evidence could become known
to the public. Between 2 and 14 to 19 May it raises serious doubt in
many believers.

Around 1 July, a question is posed. 'Are we nothing more than
images, destined to fade out when the programme is completed?
That is, when we die?'

By 11 to 17 August there may be further strong arguments that
we are only the product of genetically programmed nervous
systems.

In turn, this may arouse intense controversy over the proposi-
tion that, since we are 'pre-programmed' by our genetic inheritance, we cannot be held responsible for our actions. Many

faiths may feel threatened at this time. Such a belief could strike at the heart of an ordered society.

This prediction heralds a period when science will start to provide answers to many fundamental questions posed by the existence, not only of life, but the universe itself.

Traditional religion may feel itself to be under acute attack from such discoveries and the establishment may attempt to suppress such knowledge.

Such attempts will fail. Religious belief may have to make many adjustments in drawing closer to an understanding with the new science.

BRITISH COMMANDEER YUGOSLAV HOTELS

Les forces armées britanniques, plusieurs blessés, se logent aux hotels. C'est à fendre l'âme de voir les habitantes Yougoslaves, autrefois, tenant les mains.

British armed forces, many of them wounded, are billeted in hotels. It is heartbreaking to see women inhabitants of the former Yugoslavia holding their hands.

As early as 12 February, members of the British forces in Yugoslavia could be wounded in clashes between warring factions. British troops were despatched to Yugoslavia in 1992 to protect aid convoys, but increased fighting during the early part of 1994 could stimulate a plan for full-scale European intervention on a massive scale.

The situation in Yugoslavia worsens between 12 and 17 April, while in Britain the growing knowledge that many British soldiers could become casualties in an all-out struggle to secure peace will produce a sombre mood.

During 2 to 17 May large forces could be despatched to areas of the former Yugoslavia, while around 11 July many of them will be billeted in villages and towns. During 2 to 17 August they could have taken over many large hotels used by tourists in more peaceful times.

Between 1 and 17 September fighting could be severe, with many wounded. From 11 to 15 October British forces are holding out against great pressure. November could see a serious situation developing.

THATCHER QUITS HOUSE OF LORDS

Bredouille Margaret, la Dame de Fer, quitte la noblesse à l'intention d'entrer encore une fois la chambre des Communes à bans – là seoir à part d'un soulevement.

Empty-handed, Margaret, the Iron Lady, leaves the nobility with the intention of once more entering the Commons to cheers – there to become part of an uprising.

Surely one of the most remarkable predictions for 1994! From 1979 to 1990 Margaret Thatcher became a political legend, overseeing the restoration of market principles in the British economy and thereby influencing the direction of many other countries throughout the world. The many events during her premiership, notably the Falklands War, the 'boom' in Britain during the Eighties, the collapse of communism in Eastern Europe and the invasion of Kuwait by Saddam Hussein must mark her period of office as one of the most extraordinary in history.

In 1990, joined in a party leadership battle with Michael Heseltine, she resigned when it became clear that she would not win on a second ballot. John Major went on to win the contest, with Michael Heseltine as a member of his Cabinet.

In 1992, following a fourth consecutive Conservative victory in the April election, she took her seat in the House of Lords.

But the story, it appears, is by no means over.

There is still a vociferous Right wing in the party which advocates her principles and speaks out against the government, particularly on the divisive question of Europe. Many voters in the country still desire the return of 'the Queen over the water'.

In 1994 their wish may begin to be granted.

She leaves the Lords 'empty-handed' without the traditional symbol of the aristocracy – a sword. She will renounce her peerage to qualify once more for entry into the House of Commons. In order to do so, she will first have to fight a by-election and win it. When she does win it – as the prediction indicates – she will join and probably lead a group within the Conservative party dedicated to restoring Thatcherite principles.

From 2 January there could be a movement to persuade her to return to the Commons and around 18 February she may even renounce her peerage, although this could happen later in the year.

During 11 to 23 March she could actually have won a by-election and be entering the Commons to the cheers of her supporters. Alternatively, this period may reflect her decision to attempt such a course of action.

Between 2 and 22 April the 'Iron Lady' becomes a title much used by the press and it could be at this time that she finally leaves the House of Lords.

During 11 to 18 May there could be a revolt in the House of Lords over a proposed measure by the government.

Around 11 August the focus could be on the House of Commons, although MPs will be on holiday.

The key date of 17 November marks a decisive point, perhaps connected with electoral success.

Margaret Thatcher hits the headlines on 6 December.

VICTORIA WOOD – TV SERIES

L'anglaise acteur Victoria Wood fait une série à la télévision au sujet de sénescence. Misera le thème de tendresse par la famille, bien merité de ses bans.

The English actor Victoria Wood makes a television series on growing old. It will have a tender family theme, well deserving of its applause.

Between 2 January and 11 February the project for this television series may begin to take shape.

Possibly Victoria Wood may not write it, but she could be offered a leading role. This would account for her being called an actor, rather than a comedian, and may mark a turning point in her career. Alternatively, this could be a documentary series.

Between 6 and 15 March she could begin filming. From 2 to 16 April it could become clear that she is giving an extraordinarily tender and sensitive interpretation to the role.

The series could be televised as early as 17 to 23 May, with many plaudits and the critical view that it gives a true picture of English life. The series could be sold overseas.

Around 17 August, its themes may find their way into social discussion, possibly being used politically.

During 2 to 17 October there could be an announcement of a second series, perhaps this time extending to different themes of family life. Production could begin on 11 October.

DECEMBER

Europe Leases British Rail • Barbaric America •
The Yorks Withdraw from Royal Life •
Foxhunting Ends in Political Bribe • The English
in France • Compounds Degrade Three Times
Faster • Australian Aborigines – International
Outcry

EUROPE LEASES BRITISH RAIL

Le Rail Britannique – apparemment un fossile des jours précédents – devient isolé des autres systèmes européens. Leur allant sera mettre en baux de lignes.

British Rail – seemingly a fossil of former days – becomes isolated from the other European systems. Their energy will be put into the leasing of lines.

Evidently British Rail – falling far behind in modern rail technology used by other European systems – will find renewal by leasing lines to various European rail organisations. This could represent a break with previous government policy not to lease the lines to foreign companies. Such a development could be linked with the need for a fast rail route from the Channel Tunnel to London.

Sixth of January begins the year with a harking-back by British Rail to former days of glory, perhaps with an exhibition or promotion.

But 2 to 11 February sees the necessity of offering the leasing of lines becoming an issue.

During 1 to 11 April sees the possibility of a fossilised British Rail being newly energised by a foreign input of technological know-how. Between 1 and 6 May some major British Rail lines could be run by other organisations. Around 11 June famous lines could go European.

The future of lines not leased becomes an issue around 11 September. They may be severely restricted financially. From 12 to 17 October less lucrative lines could be leased off to local organisations willing to run them.

BARBARIC AMERICA

En l'Amerique autres communautés sont ennemis des gens qui viennent de Californie après séisme. Comme bêtes barbares, les assaillent, brulent, balayent.

In America other communities are hostile to people coming from California after the earthquake. Like wild beasts they attack, burning and sweeping them aside.

This is a prediction of a community driven wild under enormous stresses, where the fabric of society is splitting apart and the common humanity of person to person is swept aside by the sheer weight of numbers.

Twenty-six million people live in California – the most densely populated state in America. Because of seismic and economic catastrophe predicted for the state during this decade many hundreds of thousands of Californians, pehaps more, will wander like refugees through their own country, often being turned aside with violence.

For this is no longer 'boom' America, where each generation is richer than the one before. Every community will be struggling to survive. America's domestic nightmare will overshadow all else.

Between 1 February and 17 March bush fires break out without warning in California. Ruined communities may build fires in the rubble of the streets. Violence could break out between different communities.

During the period between 6 and 17 April many Californians will wander looking for another home, but they are swept aside by communities they try to enter. From 17 to 22 May these communities may resort to increased violence to prevent 'strangers' coming in.

Between 11 July and 11 September there could be an official or religious movement to stem the violence, to persuade other towns and cities to take them in. 'Who are these people, if not our own?' But this mood, beset by economic adversity, will not last.

During 15 to 17 October a powerful earthquake could occur. People fleeing will find no welcome elsewhere. Certainly, California will be subject to powerful aftershocks for years.

This grim scenario may, however, prove to be a turning point for a divided Europe.

In postwar years America has become 'the policeman of the

world', able, because of her enormous wealth, to intervene in any international 'hot spot'. Furthermore, this wealth supported political regimes and many organisations to which she was committed. NATO, for one, could not function without America.

Now the world will experience her abrupt withdrawal from foreign policy, probably for many years. The impact will be profound. Twice in this century America has been drawn into a world war beginning in Europe. Her postwar foreign policy has been dedicated to preventing this happening again by being deeply involved in European affairs.

Now, just at a time when a grave conflict is occurring in central Europe, America will be absent. The prospect of what may happen will so appal many European leaders that they will have to sink their differences and act together to prevent a third world war. Two predicted results of this forced unity will be the new supremacy of the European parliament and European military intervention to stop the civil war in Yugoslavia.

THE YORKS WITHDRAW FROM ROYAL LIFE

Pour un amour de ses cinq enfants Sara Ferguson, Duchesse de York, et son mari, le prince Andrew, font ensemble une vie separée du reste de la famille royale.

For the sake of their five children Sarah Ferguson, Duchess of York, and her husband Prince Andrew together make a life separate from the rest of the Royal Family.

Nineteen ninety-two saw huge pressures on the Royal Family, including the separation of the Prince and Princess of Wales, the divorce and remarriage of Princess Anne, and the separation of the Duke and Duchess of York during the April general election.

Andrew and Sarah will mend their marriage and go on to have another three children, after the Princesses Beatrice and Eugènie. They will become a much more private couple, while still carrying out some royal duties.

Between 2 and 18 February their reconciliation could take place, while around 11 March the focus could be on Prince William, with an announcement that he is to become Prince of Wales.

Since he is no longer in the direct line to the throne, Prince Andrew may decide on 2 April to withdraw from much contact with the Royal Family. A private agreement with his brother, the King, will gradually become known. His departure could become public between 1 and 19 May, with an announcement that the Duchess is expecting their third child. Around 11 August Sarah could be in the headlines.

Tenth of December could indicate a birth. One child may be born in 1994, another in 1995 and the fifth in 1997.

N.B. The system decodes the name 'Sara', even though it is spelt 'Sarah'.

FOXHUNTING ENDS IN POLITICAL BRIBE

La campagne contre la chasse au renard et les autres activités semblables creuse leur fosse quand il semble que ministres les offrent comme un pot-de-vin.

The campaign against foxhunting and other similiar activities digs their grave when it turns out that ministers offer them as a bribe.

Animal hunting becomes a political trophy not just once, but throughout the year. Predictions have highlighted the government's difficulties in parliament during 1994.

Government opposition to a ban on fox and other forms of hunting could persuade Tory 'back-woodsmen' to vote for the government, who will be accused of hypocrisy in bartering the lives of animals for its unpopular measures.

Alternatively, a ban on hunting is offered to 'liberal' Conservative MPs to persuade them to vote in the government lobby.

Between 11 and 17 February the government may offer political inducements on certain forms of hunting, such as hare coursing – but not foxhunting.

Between 2 and 22 March the rise of a formidable public campaign against animal hunting may force the government to offer a further inducement around 17 March.

In April, the spotlight turns to foxhunting (1 to 13 April) with considerable success, so that a further government concession occurs around 15 May.

Between 2 July and 11 August hunting is a dominant issue, while around 17 September the government could offer to ban all animal hunting. Tenth of December could mark the effective date of such a ban.

THE ENGLISH IN FRANCE

Les anglais qui ont venus à vivre à la campagne francaise y tissent une communauté nouvelle à la bobine que refuse les lueurs de la ville. Ses tertres sèmes.

The English who have come to live in the French countryside weave a new community there with a bobbin that rejects the city lights. Their burial mounds scattered.

A strange haunting prediction suggesting more than it states. English people found a community in the heart of the French countryside, perhaps developing weaving skills and other crafts for self-support.

Several communities may 'bury' themselves in the countryside, only visiting towns to sell wares. They will probably have strong ecological convictions. Many such exiles will live and die in France, never to return to England.

Between 15 January and 6 February a large group of people of similar views may reject modern life and what many regard as harsh, uncaring principles.

During 2 to 17 March they may travel to the French countryside and found a large village. Around 17 April the group could begin to farm sheep for the purpose of producing yarn for weaving.

From 17 May to 22 July this community could be in the headlines. Around 19 September publicity may cause several such communities to be founded.

From 2 October these communities begin weaving fabric (perhaps a metaphorical, as well as a literal, statement).

COMPOUNDS BIODEGRADE THREE TIMES FASTER

Mil des composés dégradables – ils décomposent à tripler le taux antérieur. Effet de l'assemblage est si fort qu'on les quète à barrer. On ne ménage pas l'issue.

One thousand degradable compounds – they decompose at triple the former rate. The series is so effective that it is sought to bar them. The issue is not carefully handled.

This is one of the two predictions for 1994 (the other being the discovery of nuclear fusion in June) giving cause for hope that great problems of modern society – in this case ecological pollution by chemical compounds – will be solved. Vested interests may try to prevent their use.

By 1 March the first of these compounds may exist and by 2 to 11 April a range of such biodegradables decomposing at triple their former rate could be developed. A range of plastic materials that break down rapidly becomes available, thereby avoiding much poisoning of the environment.

Between 6 and 21 April there could be a series of announcements and publicity surrounding the 1000 compounds and the major effect they will have on society.

During the period between 2 and 23 May there could be fierce resistance to these new compounds from those companies who may be forced out of the market. Calls for a ban may come around 17 June.

From 2 to 13 July there could be much heated debate from both sides, while government policy on this subject is viewed as confused and insensitive.

Around 17 September the question of where the government stands on ecological pollution could have become an emotive public issue. Twelfth of December could point to a decision either way.

AUSTRALIAN ABORIGINES – INTERNATIONAL OUTCRY

Le gouvernement d'Australie est sensible à critique international à propos de son traitement des aborigènes. D'emblée, issue un bulletin, un réflet blasé.

The Australian government is sensitive to international criticism in connection with its treatment of the aborigines. Right away it issues a report, an indifferent reflection.

International criticism focusing on the condition of Australian aborigines could be voiced around 12 to 15 February.

The report which the Australian government issues could be discussed from 1 to 17 April, with the conclusion that it does not meet the criticisms. Around 17 to 18 the government, sensitive to the issue, could over-react.

Between 11 and 23 May it may make certain proposals which are condemned as indifferent and not dealing with the problem.

From 1 to 2 July the aborigines may make a series of political protests, or act to highlight the issue.

Between 6 and 22 October the world spotlight could be on Australia with an announcement by the government connected with treatment of the aborigines.

SCIE
REPA

SARAH ANGLISS
WILLIAM VANDYCK

Illustrated by David Farris

Hodder
Children's
Books

a division of Hodder Headline Limited

Hodder Children's Books
A division of Hodder Headline Limited
338 Euston Road
London NW1 3BH

CONTENTS

To Ray,
May your strong, beautiful, hilarious beam
shine for ever. With scientifically
unquantifiable amounts of love, Dad.

To Gwyneth May Hughes,
with love, Sarah.

There are various quizzes in this book.
The answers can be found on pages 123-125.

INTRODUCTION

THE BIG QUESTION: WHY BOTHER WITH SCIENCE?

Yeah, why bother?

My brother?

Because . . .

FACT 1

Science is interesting
and a bit of a laugh.

Don't go!

OK! OK! We'll come back to that one. There's another point here.

FACT 2

You don't want
to look STUPID.

INTRODUCTION

Here's the scene.

You're relaxing with friends. Maybe with someone you want to impress. And maybe there's an irritating person there, showing off about how much they know that you don't. And the irritating person starts asking you questions.

What makes the sky blue?

Where do trees come from?

Why does cabbage smell so bad?

Why do your eyes close when you sneeze?

What is the point of ties?

Why are you looking irritated?

There's only one thing to do about this. Follow the First Rule of Life: "Know things: look cool." Also known as, "Don't look STUPID."

Science looks at what really happens. So just for a laugh, let's look at a few things that aren't true first.

BIG FIBS ABOUT SCIENCE

Most of us don't know any scientists, except perhaps the odd
teacher. Sometimes, the very odd teacher, like Mr E. Thick of
Sprocket School. So, anyway, it's not really surprising that some of
our ideas about science are not true. For example:

BIG FIB NO. 1

All scientists look like this . . .

Actually, you should know that this is a silly fib made up by people
who write comedy. They are trying to be "funny". They deliberately
and unfairly poke fun at scientists. This is for cheap laughs, when
frankly they ought to be just a little bit more respectful, given all the
good that scientists have done. Actually, scientists look like the one
over the page . . .

The Scientist's Union Say: No! No! Stoppit! It's not true!
Look, scientists are normal, right? Just normal people.
And anyone who says different will take part in a little
"experiment" of ours, okay?

Oh dear. Let's try another big fib instead then.

BIG FIB NO. 2

All science is very difficult.

True? False. If you've a nagging worry that this one might be true, try this simple experiment.

EXPERIMENT NO. 1: THE SOCK EXCHANGE

- Run around in some socks and shoes until you are really sweaty.
- Take both socks off then sniff them. How do they smell?
- Now put the socks in separate plastic bags, one in the freezer and one in a drawer.
- Leave them for three hours then smell them again. Which one would you rather use as a pillow case?

Now that wasn't hard, was it? But it was science. It was a genuine scientific experiment.

BIG FIB NO. 3

Scientists know all the answers.

If you believe this one, here's another experiment for you to try:

EXPERIMENT NO. 2: DIAL A SCIENTIST

Ring up your nearest university, biscuit factory, space station or government and ask to speak to their top scientist. When you get through, ask any one of the following questions:
- Is there life on another planet?
- Which numbers will win next week's lottery?
- Where do flies go in winter?

BIG FIB NO. 4

Scientists have no sense of humour.

See the results of experiment no. 2.

INTRODUCTION

Now it's time for some true points. And there is some good news.

GOOD NEWS 1

You will have noticed we didn't call the Sock Exchange "An investigation into the odour of inner foot garments as a function of mean ambient temperature."

Science is well known for using complex, technical language (jargon) that often only makes sense to other scientists. But in this book we'll be avoiding jargon as much as possible.

> It's an agricultural material repositioning device.

GOOD NEWS 2

And you are not alone.

There's the regular Repair Kit crew who will be trying to help out. As well as Mr Clevertrousers, there's Zelda . . .

> Hi! I don't know much about Science yet, but I soon will!

Then there's Colin . . .

> Hi! All you need to know about me is
>
> **TOO DULL FOR HUMAN READING**

And there's Steven, the Stupid Monster.

> I'm not stupid, I'm just . . . what was the question again?

Okay. Let's go.

ON THE GO

Okay, so you know a car can go faster than a snail (unless there's a traffic jam). But even Steven could have told you that. If you really want to work out how fast something is moving, you need to measure its speed.

Of course you've heard of speed before. It's the thing that people worry about when they're driving a car. Speed tells you how far something will move in a given amount of time.

Colin, for instance, is driving at a steady 20 kilometres per hour. 'Per' is a word you see a lot, it simply means 'every'. So Colin moves 20 kilometres further up the road every hour.

In 1 hour, he'll be exactly 20 kilometres away.
In 2 hours, he'll be 2 x 20 kilometres away. That's 40 kilometres.
In 3 hours, he'll be 3 x 20 kilometres away. That's 60 kilometres.
In 4 hours, he'll be 4 x 20 kilometres away. That's 80 kilometres.

Look at the signpost in the above picture. In 4 hours, Colin will be wishing he'd braked a little earlier!

Ah yes. It pays to know about how to deal with speed, time and distance together.

WORKING OUT SPEED

The speed of something, the distance it travels and the time it takes to get there are very neatly linked. If you know the values of two of these things, it's easy to work out the third.

To find out the distance something has travelled, multiply its speed by the time it has been moving.

speed x time = distance

Steven, for instance, is walking at 2 kilometres per hour. So in 4 hours, he will get 2 x 4 kilometres further down the road. That's 8 kilometres.

> Just so long as I can remember... it's left, right, left, right, left, right, left . . . then what?

To find the speed of something, divide the distance it has travelled by the time it has taken to get there.

speed = $\dfrac{\text{distance}}{\text{time}}$

If Colin takes 3 hours to cycle 12 kilometres, then he is cycling at $\dfrac{12}{3}$ kilometres per hour. That's 4 kilometres per hour.

4 kilometres per hour. Faster than a speeding bullet.

22223113112111322111

HANDY SPACE SAVER

Before we run out of paper and ink, Mr Clevertrousers would like to show you a shorter way of writing down the measurements of distance, time or speed.

If you write kilometres as **km**, per as **/** and hours as **h**, you can write kilometres per hour as **km/h**. The / looks like a dividing line, so it's a handy reminder that speed is distance divided by time.

Colin, for instance, was travelling at 4 km/h. He's travelling at 0 km/h now though, as he's stopped to take a rest.

We'll take Mr Clevertrousers' advice and use this handy space saver from this point onwards in the book:

km   kilometres
/   per
h   hour

80 km/h. Faster than a cycling tortoise.

13

CHOOSING YOUR UNITS

Tumbling to Earth, this piece of
space junk is going to hit the
ground at an awesome 90 000 km/h.

Let's hope it doesn't
hit this poor old snail.

He's moving an awful lot slower than the cosmic trash that's hurtling
towards him. In an hour, he will only have moved 3 centimetres. It's
easiest to write his lowly speed in centimetres per hour (cm/h).

To work out speeds, you can measure distance and time any way
you like. But remember to stick to the same units throughout your
work. If you jump from metres per second to kilometres per hour,
for instance, you could end up in an awful muddle.

This little beauty can do up to
10000 cm per minute.

Don't buy it, that's only 6 km/h!

COLIN'S TIP

To save themselves from getting into a muddle,
scientists usually stick to metres per second
(m/s) when they are measuring speed.

Whatever you do, always remember to write down your units with
your number. If you just say 'I was doing 20', no one will know
what you mean.

20 kilometres per hour? 20 metres per second? 20 furlongs per
century? 20 press ups at a time?

SPEED CHALLENGE

Don't panic! This is a quiz about speed – not a quiz you must do speedily.

Can you fill in the gaps in this chart? Take care with the units as well as the numbers!

Distance travelled	Time taken	Speed
10 kilometres	2 hours	...... km/h
15 centimetres	3 hours	...... cm/h
30 metres	10 seconds	...... m/s
16 metres	4 hours	4 ......
12 kilometres	4 seconds	3 ......
20 centimetres	5 seconds	4 ......
18 metres	3 hours	....
1 kilometre	1 second	....
24 kilometres	3 hours	....

SPEEDING UP

Colin is in a hurry. He needs to cycle home from the library before he misses *Neighbours*. Otherwise he won't know if one character is still cross with the other one, or whatever's happening on that programme at the moment. Anyway, to get home sooner, Colin starts peddling faster. This accelerates (speeds up) the bike.

Acceleration tells you how rapidly something is speeding up. You are accelerating more if you speed up more quickly.

When Colin was thinking about *Neighbours*, he was cycling at 10 m/s.

1 second later, he's cycling at 15 m/s

2 seconds later, he's cycling at 20 m/s

3 seconds later, he's cycling at 25 m/s

4 seconds later, he's cycling at 30 m/s

Colin's frantic peddling is increasing his speed by 5 m/s every second. In other words, it is making him accelerate by 5 metres per second per second. You can write this as 5 m/s/s (or 5 m/s^2).

You can work out how much something is accelerating if you remember this:

acceleration = $\dfrac{\text{change in speed}}{\text{time taken to change}}$

When Zelda the Astronaut fires the boosters on her rocket, her speed increases from 100 m/s to 280 m/s in only 3 seconds. That's an increase of 180 m/s.

As it took 3 seconds to make this change, her acceleration is $\dfrac{180}{3}$ m/s. That's 60 m/s/s.

Now, speed and acceleration are not the same thing. If one person is accelerating more than another, it doesn't mean they're going any faster.

FOX
speed 1 m/s
acceleration 2 m/s/s
the fox is getting faster so will
soon catch up with the hare.

HARE
speed 4 m/s
acceleration 0 m/s/s
the hare is running at a
steady speed.

So, the hare is in trouble.

PICK THE WINNER

These figures show what happens when three racing drivers step on the gas. Fill in the gaps to work out how much each one accelerates. Which driver has the most acceleration? Is this driver in the fastest car? Who has the broken accelerator?

	Old speed	New speed	Change in speed	Time taken to change speed	Acceleration
A	20 m/s	50 m/s	..... m/s	5 s	..... m/s/s
B	0 m/s	44 m/s	..... m/s	4 s	..... m/s/s
C	120 m/s	220 m/s	..... m/s	10 s	..... m/s/s
D	60 m/s	60 m/s	..... m/s	2 s	..... m/s/s

COLIN'S CHALKBOARD CONCLUSIONS

Speed: how fast something is travelling.

Acceleration: how fast it is changing speed.

Scientists measure speed in metres per second (m/s).

They measure acceleration in metres per second per second (m/s/s).

Accelerator

A celery eater

18

FEEL THE FORCE

Isn't it great when you kick a football really hard? And isn't it annoying when you get whacked high into the air by the Large Hammer of the Beast of Zarg?

In fact, these things have something in common. They are examples of one of the Laws of the Universe in action. And not the law that says "Whilst kicking a football can be fun, being hit by a hammer is often not", which has now fallen into disuse.

No, an altogether different law. This one tells us what happens to things when they are pushed or pulled.

Scientists call a 'push' or a 'pull' a force. One of their most important laws about forces goes like this:

If something is standing still, only a force can make it move . . .

Force

. . . and if something is moving, only a force can change its speed or the way that it's going.

Stop!

No force, no effect on movement.

FEEL THE FORCE

If all that stuff about pushing and pulling seemed obvious, it's not surprising. After all, you've been pushing, pulling and feeling forces every day of your life. Of course, people and animals aren't the only things that can push or pull. Many other things can create forces too. Some of these can be very useful:

Spring

A spring makes a force when you squash it. The more you squash it, the bigger this force becomes. As soon as you let go of a squashed spring, it grows back to its original size.

The force of this spring opens the lid of the jack-in-a-box . . .

Sorry, I thought you said "Yak in a box."

Elastic band

An elastic band makes a force when you stretch it. If you stretch it more, you make a bigger force.

When Zelda releases the elastic band of her catapult, it shrinks back to its original size. As it shrinks, it forces ammunition into the air.

Magnet

Colin has steel fillings, so a magnet will attract them.

Let's see how fixed those fillings are, then.

Mmm, not bad.

IT'S THE LAW

What's this about Laws of the Universe?

When scientists notice that something is always true, they write it down and call it a law. This helps them to think clearly about what's going on. Scientific laws don't have to be about anything tricky. In fact, they often describe things that are really obvious.

Maybe these laws will show you what I mean:

Balls roll downhill.

Ice turns into water if you make it warm enough.

Heat always flows from a hot thing to a cold thing.

Friends are more likely to telephone when you are in the bath.

Actually, that last one is a good example of something that is not really a law. Things seem that way, but it is not necessarily true.

SPACE TRIPS

The good thing about forces is that they work the same way anywhere in the universe. If you understand how they affect things on Earth, you're going to find it pretty easy to imagine what they will do in space. Zelda the Astronaut would now like to demonstrate.

Here's Zelda on board her rocket. She's 750 million kilometres from Earth at the moment, cruising out of the solar system.

PLUTO 5 000 000 000km
EARTH 750 000 000km

Zelda's rocket is going amazingly fast. She'll be passing the planet Pluto in just a few hours. But look at the back of it: there's no smoke or flames. That's because Zelda isn't running her rocket engines. So why doesn't her rocket grind to a halt?

Well, take another look at her rocket. It isn't being held back to Earth by a long elastic band. Nor is it being pulled towards a giant magnet on Mars. There's no alien spacecraft shoving it off course. In fact, Zelda's rocket isn't having to deal with any outside forces at all. That's why it is moving continually at a steady speed, without any help from her rocket engines. It won't speed up, slow down or change direction until something gets in the way.

Of course, the rocket did need to use its engines to get off the launch pad. That's because it needed to overcome its home planet's force of gravity (see pages 31–41). But next time you need to draw a rocket travelling through empty space, remember: there's no need for any smoke or flames out the back.

If you draw your rocket like this:

you'll look very, very silly.

LONG-DISTANCE MESSENGER

Launched from Earth in 1977, Voyager 1 and 2 were probes that were used to explore the planets of the solar system. When they had finished their work, there was nothing around to slow them down. That's why they carried on drifting out of the solar system and into the further reaches of space.

Voyager 1 and 2 will keep moving in a straight line and at the same speed until they hit a planet, a star or a space rock. This could be in millions of years from now. Scientists have put a special note inside each of them, just in case an alien picks it up. The note is a message of peace from planet Earth.

ROAD TRIPS

Zelda will be returning home in an hour, so Colin has gone to meet her at the spaceport.

Colin doesn't want to be late, so he's travelling at top speed. That's around 90 km/h. The engine of his motorbike has to work really hard to keep him going this fast. Colin's worried that he might run out of petrol before he gets to the spaceport.

Wait a minute! Why does Colin need to run his motorbike engine to keep going at a steady speed? I thought forces acted in the same way everywhere in the universe. In space, Zelda didn't need to run her rocket engine at all.

Don't worry! There's nothing fishy going on. Forces do act the same way wherever you are. But Zelda's situation is different to Colin's. Remember: her rocket didn't have to deal with any outside forces. Colin's motorbike, on the other hand, does.

But there isn't an elastic band, a magnet, an alien or anything else pushing or pulling his motorbike.

True. But Colin's motorbike is experiencing another kind of force altogether. Unlike Zelda's rocket, it's moving along a road. As its rubber tyres roll over the tarmac, they create a force that makes it harder for the motorbike to go forwards. This force is called 'friction'.

If Colin switched his engine off, friction would slow his motorbike down. Eventually, it would bring him to a stop.

Here's another problem that Colin's motorbike has to deal with. Unlike Zelda's rocket, it's surrounded by air (there is no air in outer space). Air is made up of billions of tiny bits, called atoms. These bump into Colin's motorbike as he moves forward, forcing it to slow down a little more. The force they make is called **air resistance**.

Colin's engine needs to make a force that's bigger than the motorbike's air resistance and friction. Otherwise, it won't push the motorbike forwards, meaning he'll never reach the spaceport.

FEELING FRICTION

There's friction between the palms of your hands. When you rub your palms together, this turns some of the moving energy into heat and sound. That's why your palms get warmer. It's also why you can hear them rubbing together.

If you make things smoother or grease them, you lessen the friction between them. That's why people often grease the moving parts of machines.

Try covering your palms in cooking oil. Then rub them together again. Are they easier or harder to rub together? How much noise do they make when you rub them?

PUTTING ON THE BRAKES

Brakes use friction to slow wheels down. When Colin presses the brake of his motorbike, he squeezes a metal pad against a disk on his front wheel. Friction between the pad and disk slow the wheel down.

STREAMLINED

Over the years, engineers have found that some vehicles have more air resistance than others. In general, teardrop-shaped vehicles with few sharp corners create the least air resistance. These are called streamlined vehicles.

Streamlined

Not so streamlined

ACTION AND REACTION

All this stuff about forces helps to explain Colin's Unfortunate
Accident at the skateboarding park.

To his horror, as he stepped forward off the skateboard, Colin
made it shoot backwards. This caused poor Colin to lose his
balance completely and tumble ungracefully to the floor.

Now, let's have a closer look at that.

CLOSE UP

No, not that bit. This bit.

ACTION
the force
you make

REACTION
the force
this creates
in the opposite
direction

This was obviously a common accident – not surprising really when
you consider this law about forces:

When you force something to move in one direction, you also make
another force. This is just as strong as the force you originally make
– but it works in the opposite direction.

MORE FORCEFUL EXAMPLES

action

As Colin hits the tennis ball, forcing it forwards . . .

reaction

. . . the ball forces his racket to spring backwards.

action

As Steven steps off the boat towards the riverbank . . .

reaction

. . . he forces the boat to move away from the riverbank.

Note: "Every action creates an equal and opposite reaction." This is a law of science, not human nature. So beware.

MEASURING FORCE

Some pushes or pulls are much stronger than others. That's why it's so handy to measure the strength of any force.

a bit weedy   **stronger**   **very impressive**

Well that's one way to measure forces. But sometimes you may need a measurement that's a little more precise. That's when you should use **newtons**.

Roughly how big is a newton?

A newton is roughly the force you would make if you dangled an apple from the end of a spring. Two apples would stretch the spring twice as far. They'd make a force of around 2 newtons. Imagine four people pulling an enormous elephant on a rope over a pulley.

Every one of these people is pulling on this rope with a force of around 300 newtons. As there are 4 of them pulling in the same direction, they're making an overall force of around 1200 newtons (300 x 4 = 1200).

Exactly how big is a newton?

Scientists don't really use apples to gauge the size of a newton. If you're really interested, this is how they work out what a newton is exactly:

Forces slow things down or speed them up. In other words, they accelerate them.

A newton is the force that will accelerate 1 kilogram of something – tomatoes, tea trays, rocks or anything else – by 1 m/s/s. The short way to write 'newtons' is **N**.

FORCE, MASS AND ACCELERATION

If you know the mass of something and how much it's accelerating, you can work out the force that is acting on it. That's because force, mass and acceleration are linked like this:

force (in N) = mass (in kg) x acceleration (in m/s/s)

NEWTON QUIZ

Can you fill in these gaps?

1. 5 dogs, each pull with a force of 25 N. Total force .... N.

2. A force of .... N will accelerate a 2 kg bag of flour by 6 m/s/s.

3. A 15 N force is accelerating this rabbit by 3 m/s/s.
   The rabbit has a mass of .... kg.

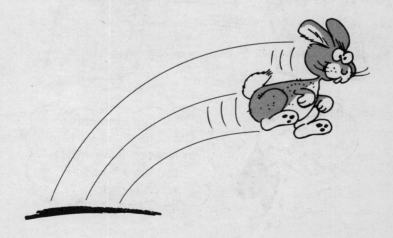

COLIN'S CHALKBOARD CONCLUSIONS

CHANGING HOW THINGS MOVE
Only a force can make a still object move. Only a force can change the speed of an object or the direction in which it's travelling.

FRICTION
This force makes it harder for things to slide or roll over each other. If you make things smoother or cover them in oil, you reduce the friction between them.

AIR RESISTANCE
This force makes it harder for things to move through air.

ACTION AND REACTION
Every action force makes a reaction force. This is just as strong as the action force but works in the opposite direction.

MEASURING FORCES
Forces are measured in newtons (N). 1 N is roughly the force an apple makes when you dangle it.
Force (in N) = mass (in kg) x acceleration (in m/s/s).

How can I remember that the short version of Newton is N? I know, the word 'Newton' actually ends in N.

DOWN TO EARTH

Oi, you! Question.

If a mouse and an elephant jump off the side of a high cliff into the sea, who will hit the water first?

The Elephant is heavier, so it must be the elephant. And yet . . . I have a sneaky feeling that something is not quite right . . .

Correct! They hit the water together.

To understand why they get there together, you have to know a little bit more about the force that's pulling them downwards. It's something we feel all the time while we are on Earth: the force of **gravity**.

WHAT IS GRAVITY?

Life would be very different if there was no force of gravity.

Shopping would be much easier to carry home.

Hairdos would be
more daring.

Football would be a far more challenging game.

Oh yes – and the air and oceans wouldn't stick to the planet, you
wouldn't need your heart to pump blood around your body, the
Earth would no longer orbit the Sun . . . you get the general idea.

Gravity is a force that pulls things together. It will pull together any
two things that have a mass.

Earth has a mass (a really big one – around 600 million million
billion kilograms) and so do you. That's why gravity continually
pulls you towards the centre of the Earth.

Earth's gravity keeps your feet on the ground, your shopping in its
basket and your hair pointing downwards – most of the time.

GREAT UNKNOWN FACTS OF THE HISTORY OF SCIENCE. PART 12.

Sir Isaac "Lucky" Newton

. . . was not, in fact, the first person to understand gravity when an apple fell on his head.

He certainly made his breakthrough famous.

But the first person to discover gravity was actually Sir Isaac's brother, the less well known Mr Ian "Unlucky" Newton.

DOWN TO EARTH

WHAT DOES GRAVITY DO?

Just like any other force, the force of gravity accelerates things. On Earth, it accelerates them towards the ground.

You don't feel this acceleration when you're standing on something. That's because whatever you are standing on stops you moving downwards.

But you do feel it when there's nothing under your feet.

Earth's gravity creates a downwards acceleration of just under 10 m/s/s. In case you're interested, the exact acceleration is closer to 9.8 m/s/s. But this figure varies from place to place. It's ever so slightly lower at the peaks of high mountains, for example, as these are further from the centre of the Earth. (The force of gravity is weaker between things that are further apart.)

Now this acceleration is the same for everything – whether it's as heavy as a mouse, an elephant or an armoured truck. That's why objects will always hit the ground (or the sea) together if they fall from the same height.

So, as long as I keep falling, the weight will never catch up with me.

But what about the things I learned on my last sky diving course? When I jump out of the aeroplane, I spread out my body so I don't speed up too much while I'm falling.

Gravity is still working when you are sky diving. If it wasn't for the air around you, it would make you accelerate at just under 10 m/s/s, just like any other falling object. But when you spread your body out, you become far less streamlined. You make lots of air resistance that stops you from building up as much speed while you fall.

A parachute has an even bigger effect. It's so unstreamlined, lots of air collects inside its open canopy. It's very hard for the canopy to cut through this air, so it never reaches a very high speed.

That's why you float gently to the ground.

GRAVITY QUIZ

Read the last couple of pages **very carefully** then see if you can fill in the blanks:

The Great Torino weighs 70 kg. When he jumps off the trapeze, he falls with an acceleration of 9.8 m/s/s.

His wife, Mighty Torina, only weighs 35 kg. When she jumps off the trapeze, she falls with an acceleration of ..... m/s/s.

Their cat also jumps off the trapeze. He only weighs 10 kg. He falls with an acceleration of ..... m/s/s.

On seeing the dog, several mice also jump from the trapeze. Each mouse weighs only 0.1 kg. They fall with an acceleration of ...... m/s/s.

IS THERE GRAVITY IN SPACE?

Yes, there it is! Let's take a closer look at some astronauts at work.

ON THE MOON
Here are a couple of Zelda's friends, Neil and Buzz, on the Moon.

Neil and Buzz are certainly finding it easy to skip around the Moon, even with their heavy spacesuits on. But when they jump up off the Moon's surface, they do come back down again gently.

There is a force of gravity on the Moon. Remember: gravity exists between any two things that have mass. Because the Moon is so much lighter than Earth, the Moon's gravity is about six times smaller than the Earth's. Astronauts, rocks, hammers, feathers and anything else near the surface of the Moon will accelerate downwards at only 1.6 m/s/s. That's why Neil and Buzz stay on the Moon's surface but find it easy to get around.

IN EMPTY SPACE

Well what about these aliens? They're no where near a planet or moon. Their spaceship is parked in empty space, halfway between Venus and Jupiter.

As they're such a long way from the surface of any planet, they don't experience a strong force of gravity. But they still feel the force of gravity from planets in the distance. They are far away from these planets, so the force of gravity they feel is very weak. However, it's still strong enough to gently pull loose objects around the cabin. If any crew members lose a screwdriver, a cuddly toy or a hairbrush, they can find it the next morning on one wall of the spaceship.

GRAVITY EVERYWHERE

Amazingly, there are tiny forces of gravity between you and each of your friends, your bed, your neighbour's dog and this book. That's because you, your friends and all these objects have a mass. Of course, these forces are so small, they're swamped by all the other forces around you – especially the force of Earth's gravity. That's why you never feel giddy.

Oh, Colin, that's a different kind of attraction, not one that scientists have to worry about very much. Unlike Robin here. He's a top researcher at the Laboratory of Love.

THE DIFFERENCE BETWEEN MASS AND WEIGHT

If you want to spend your life in the supermarket, you don't need to learn the difference between mass and weight. At the fruit and vegetable counter, the words 'these tomatoes weigh 2 kilos' mean exactly the same as 'these tomatoes have a mass of 2 kilos'.

But if you want to take your tomatoes somewhere more exciting – to the Moon for example – you'll need to handle the words 'mass' and 'weight' with more care. Zelda would like to show you the reason why:

Here's Zelda with her favourite tomato flan. It's pretty hefty – large enough for her to feast on for a week. Zelda's flan is packed with tasty tomatoes. It has a mass of 5 kilograms.

If Zelda takes her tomato flan to the Moon, it doesn't lose any tomatoes. Nor does any pastry flake off it. It's packed with just as much food as ever, so it still has a mass of 5 kilograms.

Zelda's flan would have a mass of 5 kilograms on Venus, Mars, in empty space, at the bottom of the ocean . . . just about anywhere.

Now think about how Zelda would carry her flan. On Earth it's so heavy, she'd need both hands to carry it. But on the Moon she could balance it on the palm of one hand. In space she wouldn't need to hold it at all. The flan floats freely inside her rocket.

The flan's mass is always 5 kilograms – but something else changes when Zelda moves from place to place. This is the flan's weight.

Weight is a force that pulls things downwards. The weight of Zelda's flan depends on the force of gravity. This force is six times weaker on the Moon than on the Earth. That's why Zelda's flan is so much lighter on the Moon.

In space, the force of gravity is almost zero. That's why Zelda's flan can float.

MEASURING WEIGHT

Just like any other force, weight is measured in newtons. Remember how weight, mass and acceleration are linked (see page 29).

Mass of Zelda's flan: 5 kilograms

Acceleration due to gravity on Earth is about 9.8 m/s/s.

So the weight of Zelda's flan on Earth is about 5 x 9.8 newtons. That's roughly 49 N.

Acceleration due to gravity on the Moon is about 1.6 m/s/s.

So the weight of Zelda's flan on the Moon is about 5 x 1.6 newtons. That's roughly 8 N.

No wonder Zelda's flan seems so much lighter on the Moon.

WEIGHT QUIZ

Fill in the blanks to show how much these animals would weigh on the Earth and the Moon. Round up the figures to the nearest newton.

Animal	Mass	Weight on Earth	Weight on Moon
Rabbit	1 kg	.... N	.... N
Dog	6 kg	.... N	.... N
Polar bear	750 kg	.... N	.... N
Elephant	2000 kg	.... N	.... N

WAIT QUIZ

How long does this all go on before I can eat this wretched thing?

BALANCED FORCES

So far, you've seen how forces can change the way things move. But did you know forces can also stop things going anywhere at all?

Steven and Colin would like to show you what this means using their two-man tent.

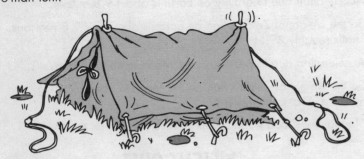

If Steven pulls on this guy rope, he forces the tent to the left.

If Colin pulls on the other one, he forces it to the right.

The tent isn't fixed to anything yet, so the slightest breeze could knock it over.

But what happens if they both pull together?

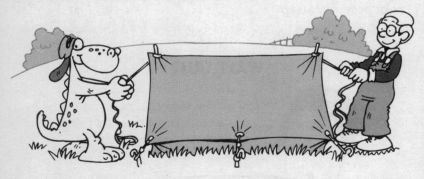

Steven and Colin are pulling in opposite directions. They are pulling just as hard as each other, so the forces they make are balanced. This is why they make the tent stand up. If they nail the stretched guy ropes in the ground, the balanced forces of the two ropes will help to keep the tent up.

OTHER EXAMPLES

This dog and its owner are pulling on the lead with the same force. That's why neither is going anywhere.

Just another 5 minutes of this exercise and we can go back home to the fire.

Gravity pulls these books downwards towards the table. As this happens, the table makes a reaction force that pushes the books upwards (see page 26). The downwards and upwards forces are exactly the same strength, so the books stay put.

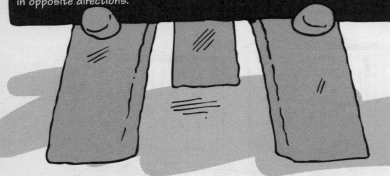

COLIN'S CHALKBOARD CONCLUSIONS

GRAVITY ON EARTH

The force of gravity pulls us towards the centre of the Earth. It's the force that keeps us on the ground.

GRAVITY EVERYWHERE

Gravity exists between any objects that have mass. Gravity is much stronger between objects that have more mass or objects that are closer together.

SIZE OF FORCE OF GRAVITY

On Earth, gravity accelerates everything downwards at about 9.8 m/s/s. The Moon is much lighter than Earth. That's why gravity on the Moon is six times smaller. It only accelerates things downwards at about 1.6 m/s/s.

MASS AND WEIGHT

The mass of an object tells you how much stuff it contains. This doesn't vary from place to place. Mass is measured in kilograms. The weight of an object tells you how much gravity is forcing it downwards. It depends on where you are. Weight is measured in newtons. Objects weigh roughly six times more on the Earth than on the Moon.

BALANCING FORCES

Two forces can stop something moving if they pull with the same strength in opposite directions.

Juggling is easy, you just throw things up into the air.

I think you fail to understand the gravity of the situation.

FULL OF ENERGY

Energy is what you need to make things happen.

For instance, things have energy when there is movement, noise, light or heat:

When they have more energy, things get faster, noisier, brighter or hotter:

43

SOUND AND LIGHT

The human body is a very good energy sensor.
Our eyes and ears, for example,
notice sound and light that reaches them.

Sound is a form of energy that we can hear.

Light is a form of energy that we can see.

If you want to enjoy sound, light, heat and
moving energy in action, there's nothing
better than a firework display.

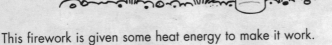

This firework is given some heat energy to make it work.

It has moving energy when it shoots up into the air.

It releases a huge burst of sound and light energy when it explodes.

Steven and Zelda cast long shadows as they watch the display. That's
because their bodies block the path of light from the fireworks.

ROUND THE BEND

Oh dear! It looks like Colin is a little nervous of the fireworks. He's decided to seek refuge behind this wall. He can no longer see the fireworks from here as light can't travel around corners. But he can certainly hear them – sound travels around corners very well.

REFLECTIONS

But wait! The surface of that shop window on the other side of the road is so smooth, light can reflect (bounce) off it perfectly, as though it were a mirror. If Colin looks into it, he can see an image of the fireworks.

Light from the fireworks also reflects off this wall. But the wall has a bumpy surface, so light bounces off it in all directions. That's why the reflection doesn't make an image.

Now I'm having a good time.

HEAT

If you've ever been out on a very cold day, you'll know all about heat energy. Colin often needs some extra heat energy when he travels on his motorbike in the middle of winter. That's why he's always so pleased to get home to his faithful dog Spike.

As soon as Colin gets home, Spike nuzzles up to him and gives him a doggy hello. Spike is much warmer than Colin, so heat flows rapidly from Spike to Colin, warming Colin up. Spike is losing heat to Colin, so he cools down. Heat keeps flowing until Colin and Spike are the same temperature.

THERMOMETERS

You can use a thermometer to measure how hot things are. The numbers on the side of thermometers measure temperature in degrees centigrade. To save space, this is written as **°C**.

Ice melts at 0°C   Water boils at 100°C.

BELOW ZERO

Melting ice is very cold but it's not the coldest thing around. The inside of a freezer, for example, is around 4°C cooler than the temperature of melting ice. In other words, it's 4°C below zero. In laboratories, scientists have been able to cool things down to around 273°C below zero. Nothing in the universe can get colder than this temperature. That's why it's called **absolute zero**.

HOT AND COLD QUIZ

Can you match each of these items to its temperature?

Colin's armpit	300 °C
cup of tea	4 °C below zero
inside of a freezer	18 °C
coldest air at the South Pole	273 °C below zero
water inside a boiling kettle	38 °C
core of the Sun	60 °C below zero
air in Zelda's flat	100 °C
air inside an oven	15 600 000 °C
coldest temperature anywhere in the universe	70 °C

ENERGY CHANGES

Energy has a funny habit of changing from one form to another. This makes some very interesting things happen. Steven would now like to demonstrate.

MOVING ENERGY INTO SOUND

When Steven hits this giant gong, he gives it some of his moving energy. This makes the gong vibrate (wobble to and fro). The vibrating gong changes this moving energy into sound. The sound spreads through the air in all directions.

HEAT INTO MOVING ENERGY

When Steven leaves this fizzy drink bottle out in the Sun, the drink heats up. As it heats, the gas inside it expands (grows in size). Eventually, it becomes so big, it blows the top off the bottle, spraying fizzy drink everywhere. The heat energy has been turned into moving energy.

ELECTRICITY INTO LIGHT

About a tenth of the electricity that flows through lightbulbs turns into light. That's why lightbulbs glow. Nine-tenths of the electricity turns into heat, making the lightbulb hot.

ENERGY STORES

Things that burn, like candlewicks, matches and petrol, are simple energy stores. They have chemical energy – energy that is stored in the materials that make them up. Burning coal, for example, turns its chemical energy into heat and light.

Even the pages of this book are simple energy stores – because you can burn them. But don't even think about it!

ALL CHANGE!

Can you spot the energy changes that are going on here?

THUNDERSTORM
Thunderstorms happen when huge bursts of electricity flow between the ground and the sky. During the storm, this electricity is turned into light (a flash of lightning) and sound (a clap of thunder). Light travels around a million times faster than sound. That's why you see lightning before you hear the thunder that goes with it.

HOW FAR?
The light from a flash of lightning travels so fast (around 300 million m/s), it reaches you almost instantly. The sound, on the other hand, travels at only 330 m/s so it takes around 3 seconds to go 1 kilometre.

Next time there's a storm, count the number of seconds between the lightning and the thunder. Divide this number by 3. This is roughly the distance of the storm from you in kilometres.

But I haven't counted to 1 yet!

COLIN'S CHALKBOARD CONCLUSIONS

WHAT IS ENERGY?
Sound, light, heat and electricity are all types of energy. Things also have energy if they are on the move.

Things are faster, noisier, brighter or hotter when they have more energy.

Energy can change from one form to another.

STORING ENERGY
Energy can be stored. Fuels like coal and oil release their stored energy when you burn them.

SOUND AND LIGHT
Sound, unlike light, can travel around ordinary corners. In air, sound travels around a million times slower than light.

SWITCHING ON

Who turned out the lights?

Oh dear! It looks like the whole town is suffering from a powercut. When this happens, you really notice how much we rely on electricity.

Steven is writing a list of all the electrical things he's used today. What's your list?

WARNING

Never play with mains electricity.

That's the electricity that comes out of sockets like these:

Mains electricity can kill!

HANDY ENERGY

Electricity is one of the most handy forms of energy around. That's because it's very easy to move electricity from place to place. You can carry it from one place to another along wires.

Wires underground carry electricity from the power station to your home.

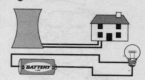

Wires inside torches carry electricity from the battery to the lightbulb.

It's also easy to store electricity until you need it. One of the simplest electricity stores is a battery. It stores electrical energy using the chemicals inside it. When you use a battery, these chemicals change and release their electrical energy.

It's also easy to change electricity into other energy forms. When you use an electric kettle, for example, you turn electricity into heat for boiling water. Here are some other electrical energy changers that you may know:

A loudspeaker turns electricity into sound.

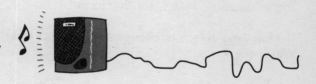

An electric fire turns electricity into heat and light. That's why it gets hot and glows.

A sewing machine turns electricity into moving energy. This energy moves the needle and thread up and down. It also turns some energy into sound. That's why the sewing machine is quite noisy.

SWITCHING ON

Fingers on buzzers, please, it's time for our

ELECTRIC QUIZ.

COLIN   ZELDA   STEVEN

That's "buzzers", Steven, not "buzzards".

The following objects all change electricity into other energy forms.
Which ones?

kettle	sound	light	(heat)	moving energy
food mixer	sound	light	heat	moving energy
lawnmower	sound	light	heat	moving energy
torch	sound	light	heat	moving energy
TV	sound	light	heat	moving energy
telephone	sound	light	heat	moving energy

MAKING A CIRCUIT

Batteries are packed with electricity.

You can't see it or smell it. You'll get a nasty shock if you try to taste it. In fact, you can't do anything useful with it until you give it somewhere to go.

Steven is completely in the dark about how to light up his bulb.

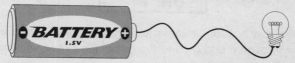

He wants electricity to flow from the battery to the bulb, so he's put a wire between them. Nothing's happening though, because the electricity can't flow.

Electricity will only flow if there's a complete path for it, out of the battery then in again. A path like this is called a **circuit**.

Luckily Colin's arrived, carrying another wire in his pocket. As soon as Colin fixes this between the other side of the bulb and battery . . . the path is complete.

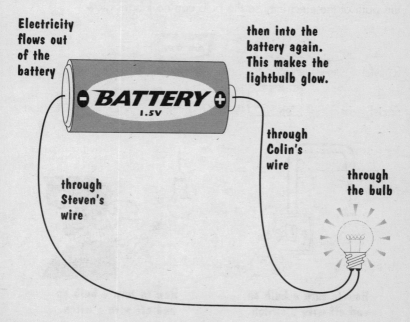

Electricity flows out of the battery

then into the battery again. This makes the lightbulb glow.

through Colin's wire

through Steven's wire

through the bulb

SWITCH

If you want an easy way to turn a bulb on and off, then you should use a switch.

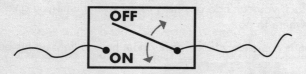

When the switch is 'on' it works just like a piece of wire. Electricity can flow through it and around the rest of the circuit, making the bulb glow.

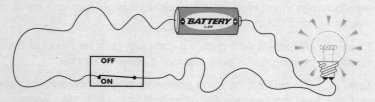

When the switch is 'off', it works just like a broken wire. It breaks the path of the electricity so the bulb can no longer glow.

How to turn a bulb on and off with a switch.

How to turn a bulb on and off with a witch.

54

MORE BULBS

There was meant to be a moonlit dance at the spaceport tonight, but the clouds are in the way. A keen partygoer, Steven hopes to rescue the party with a spectacular electric lightshow. He's bought lots of bulbs and wires as well as a brand new battery. The guests will be arriving soon, so he gets straight down to work.

Steven starts with something simple: one bulb and a battery.

The bulb glows brightly enough for Steven to see his footsteps.

Thrilled by his lightshow, Steven invites Zelda to join in the fun.

Oh dear! There seems to be a problem. Neither bulb looks as bright as Steven's did before. There's barely enough light for Zelda and Steven to see their knees.

SWITCHING ON

Colin's come along to see what's going on. Steven hopes things will improve if he adds one more bulb.

But that's made the bulbs dimmer than ever. The dancers can hardly see beyond the end of their noses.

Luckily Colin hasn't come empty handed. In his pocket, he has lots of extra batteries. When he adds two more batteries into the circuit . . .

. . . all three dancers can see their feet again.

If you're wondering why the dancers needed all those extra batteries, you'll need to take a closer look at bulbs and batteries themselves.

BULBS

There's a very skinny wire inside each bulb. Electricity finds it hard to flow through this. Electricians say the wire has a high resistance. When electricity passes through the skinny wire, it warms it and makes it glow. That's how the lightbulb turns electricity into heat and light.

BATTERIES

A battery pushes electricity around a circuit. Electricians measure the strength of its electrical push in volts.

The voltage (number of volts) is written on the side of every battery. This is a 1.5 volt battery. The rate that it pushes electricity around a circuit is called the **current**. If a battery has to push electricity through a big resistance, the current it makes will be small.

STEVEN'S FOOTLIGHTS
When Steven puts three bulbs instead of one in his circuit, the resistance of his circuit becomes three times bigger. That's because the current has to go through three lots of skinny wire inside the bulbs.

As the battery finds it three times harder to push against this resistance, the current becomes three times smaller. It's only big enough to make the bulbs glow dimly.

When Colin adds in two more batteries, he gives the electricity a bigger push. Three batteries have three times the push, so they make three times the current. Enough current flows through each bulb to make it light up a dancer's feet.

LIGHTBULB QUIZ

Look at these circuits that Colin and Zelda have built. Which one will make **each** bulb glow brightest?

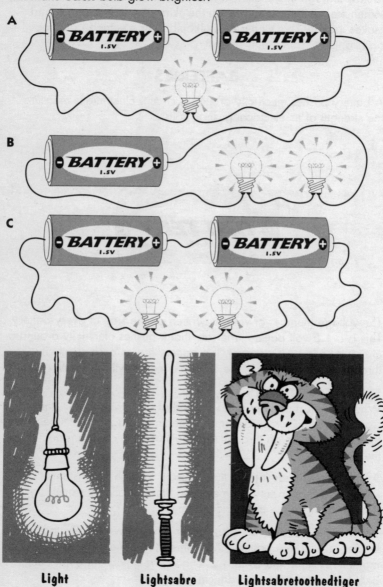

| Light | Lightsabre | Lightsabretoothedtiger |

DRAWING CIRCUITS

Colin wants to send a postcard to his auntie, telling her how much he's learnt about electricity. He thought it would be nice to send her a quick sketch showing the lightbulbs in his study. He wants to show her that he's built a circuit of a battery, light, and switch. If he had time (and an ability to draw), he'd draw this:

But he doesn't. Instead of realistic batteries, wires and switches, his diagram can use symbols.

Realistic drawings   **Circuit symbols**

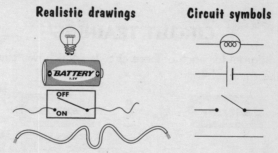

Colin doesn't need to bother drawing the clips and sticky tape that hold his circuit together. All he needs to show is the electricity's path around the circuit.

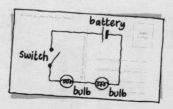

Colin's finished his circuit diagram and has five minutes to catch the post. His auntie will be very proud.

SWITCHING ON

CIRCUIT TRAINING

Draw a diagram for each of these circuits. Which two circuits do exactly the same job?

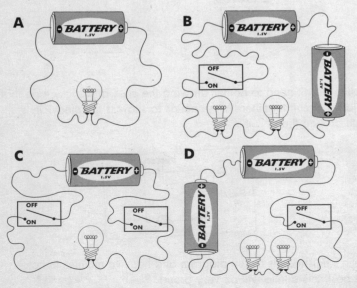

60

COLIN'S CHALKBOARD CONCLUSIONS

Electricity only flows from a battery when there is a complete circuit (path), out of the battery then in again.

Flowing electricity is called a current.

Voltage tells you how strongly a battery can push electricity around a circuit.

Skinny wires (inside bulbs for instance), have a high resistance. They make it hard for current to flow.

CIRCUIT DIAGRAMS

These don't show wobbles, twists, turns or fixings. They just show the path of electricity through a circuit.

CIRCUIT SYMBOLS

wire

battery

bulb

switch

Circuit Diagram    **Sir Cat Diagram**

MATERIALS AND THEIR PROPERTIES

Picking the right materials to do a job is very, very important.
Here are some of Steven's designs for new products. They're all
perfectly good except for the materials he's chosen to use.

Jelly Saw

String Glasses

Fish Wig

Egg Hammer

We need to think about what materials would be suitable for what
we want done.

TESTS OF STRENGTH

We all have a fairly good idea of how strong things are. For instance, you can probably guess which bridge is safer: one made of biscuits or one made of bricks.

It's often useful to know how strong a material is when you squash it – or stretch it.

But it's also essential to think about strength in other ways.

This slab of concrete, for example, can carry lots of weight without breaking. But if you bend it too far, it will snap.

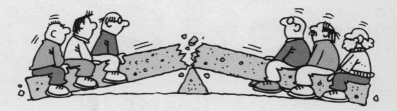

IMPORTANT ANNOUNCEMENT

So, when you're designing something like a car, a bridge or a table, you have to think very hard about how you want it to be strong. For instance, do you want it to last when people sit on it, bend it, stretch it, kick it or put it through its paces in some other way?

Engineers are very careful about the words they use when they describe materials. The word 'strong' doesn't really tell them enough. You should choose your words carefully too – or you could end up looking very silly.

GREAT UNKNOWN BITS OF MATERIALS HISTORY. PART 29: THE BUNGEE JUMP.

The real breakthrough in Bungee Jumping came in 1964 when JR Hackett realised that whilst he needed something strong, he also needed something flexible to cushion the fall of the jumper.

1870
Metal chain:
too inflexible, too painful.

1913
Chain of sausages:
too soft and food-orientated.

1943
Cheese wire:
too liable to cut one's feet off.

1964
Elastic band:
too much fun!

2000
Elastic band kept in pocket by mistake:
several accidents.

SOME INTERESTING TESTS OF STRENGTH

HARDNESS

Wood, metal and rocks are hard. Marshmallows, skin and clay are soft. If something is very hard, you need a very big force to dent it.

Hard   **Easy**   **Even easier (but not much point)**

FLEXIBILITY

This tells you how strong a material is when you bend it. A flexible material can be bent a long way without snapping. A rope is flexible – a biscuit is not. Many materials, like toffee, become more flexible when you warm them up.

> **Scientific Question waiting to be researched:**
> Is this why bananas, which grow in hot countries, are bent?

ELASTICITY

This tells you how much you can stretch something without permanently changing it. When you stretch an elastic material then let it go, it will ping back to its original size and shape.

Rubber, the stuff that's used to make elastic bands, is an elastic material (yes – some things in science are really obvious).

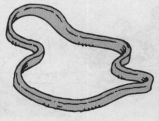

Stretchy

Hard

ADVANCED STUDENTS ONLY

TOUGHNESS

A tough material can withstand a lot of bending or twisting before it breaks. Materials that can't stand much of this are called 'brittle' materials.

Wait a minute! Don't toughness and flexibility mean the same thing?

Not exactly. If an amazingly strong giant monster bent the girders of this bridge in half, they would almost certainly snap. That's because they're not very flexible. But over the years, as millions of cars and people ride over the bridge, they bend the girders millions of times, each time by a tiny amount. The girders can stand up to this because they're very tough.

Tough Bridge

Tough, Bridge

CONDUCTORS AND INSULATORS

Pie's ready!

What do you do?

Wrong! Steven is hurt, and will be hungry when he drops the pie. Tin is made of metal, a material that heat can pass through very easily. These materials are called **conductors**.

The foam padding on ovengloves isn't just for its great stylish look. Nor is it to make them feel softer. It's there because it's an insulator – a material that hardly any heat can get through. The thicker you make the padding, the less heat can get through, so the better the oven gloves work.

SOME HEAT CONDUCTORS
Metal spoon
Earthenware mug
Disposable plastic cup
Glass window

SOME HEAT INSULATORS
Wooden spoon
Rubber soles
Polystyrene cup
Foam

ELECTRICITY

Most heat insulators are good electrical insulators too. In other words, electricity finds it difficult to pass through them. This means the same thing as having a high resistance.

FACTS SHOWING THAT ELECTRICITY AND HEAT ARE NOT THE SAME THING.

1. Unfortunately, objects that conduct heat well don't always make good electrical conductors. Heat flows very easily through an earthenware mug, for instance, but earthenware is used to make insulators on overhead power lines.

2. A TV will not work in these conditions . . .

CONDUCTOR OR INSULATOR?

An easy electrical test
Put your specimen between two crocodile clips. If it's an electrical conductor, the circuit will be complete so the bulb will light up. If it's an insulator, electricity can't flow through it, so nothing will happen — sorry.

An easy heat test
Put one end of your specimen in a hot bath. Hold the other end in your hand. If the specimen is a conductor, heat will flow through it and warm up your hand.

BURNING QUESTION

Steven is stirring a saucepan of hot food. In which of the following situations do you think Steven will burn his hand?

A. Stirring with a metal spoon.

B. Stirring with a wooden spoon.

C. Stirring with a metal spoon, but with foam padding around the saucepan.

D. Stirring with a metal spoon, but with baking foil around the handle of the spoon.

E. Stirring with a metal spoon, but with foam padding around the handle of the spoon.

SOLIDS, LIQUIDS AND GASES

Have you ever wondered why:
When your pour orange juice on to a table, it spreads out to make a nasty mess. But a book put on a table does not?
You can't smell a telephone when you walk into a room – but you can smell whatever's cooking?
Water doesn't have to fill a glass to the top – but air always fills a room to the top?

These things behave differently because they're in different states.

WHAT'S A STATE?

Every substance around you is in one of three states: solid, liquid or gas.

This ice cube, for example, is solid.
It melts to form water, a liquid.
If you boil the water, it joins the air as a gas.

TEST SPACE

You can tell if something is solid, liquid or gas by watching what happens to it when you release it into a big open room.

The solid won't change shape at all. The liquid will flow until it evenly fills the floor of the room. Some liquids flow faster than others. Water, for example, flows much faster than treacle. The gas will gradually spread out in all directions – even upwards through the room.

SOLID, LIQUID OR GAS?

Can you group these objects into solids, liquids and gases?

	Solid	Liquid	Gas
puddle	☐	☐	☐
spoon	☐	☐	☐
air	☐	☐	☐
bad breath	☐	☐	☐
soup	☐	☐	☐
sweat	☐	☐	☐
Plasticine	☐	☐	☐
honey	☐	☐	☐

FOR ADVANCED STUDENTS ONLY

THE CREEPS

Sorry! What we said about solids wasn't completely true. Some solids actually spread out, over a long time, just like liquids in slow motion. Tarmac creeps slowly in this way.

To confuse matters more, it's hard to say whether some materials are solid or liquid as they're a bit like both – or neither! Glass is like this. When glass is very hot (over 1000 degrees Centigrade), it's molten – slightly runny. Unlike ordinary liquids, this molten glass holds its shape if it's twisted, pulled or rolled into sheets. Solid glass is molten glass that has cooled.

COLIN'S CHALKBOARD CONCLUSIONS

STRENGTH
You can find out the force you need to break something when you squash or stretch it – but you can measure the strength of things in many other ways. For instance you can look at:

hardness   flexibility   elasticity   toughness

CONDUCTORS
Heat or electricity can pass through them easily.

INSULATORS
Heat or electricity finds it hard to pass through them.
A good heat conductor isn't always a good conductor of electricity.

STATES OF MATTER

Solids: don't change their shape to fill a space (unless they slowly 'creep')

Liquids: will flow to fill up the bottom of an empty space

Gases: will spread out in all directions through an empty space

Metal –
a good conductor

Wood –
not a
good conductor

Musical –
not what we
meant by conductor

CHANGING MATERIALS

What's the most wonderful thing about baking a cake?

The nice smell that wafts through the house . . .

The fact that it's cheaper than buying one from the shops . . .

Or licking the bowl when no one's looking . . .

Or is it the way that you can make a load of unappetising ingredients turn into something really delicious?

Yuk   **Yum**

Whenever you rustle something up in the kitchen, you're a materials scientist at work. Every recipe brings ingredients together to make something completely new. The kitchen is a good place to see how materials change when you heat them, cool them or bring them together.

CHANGING STATE

You can change many materials simply by changing their state. You can melt, boil, evaporate, condense or freeze them.

MELTING

When chocolate becomes warm enough, the fatty part of it melts to become a liquid. This is why the chocolate goes runny enough to pour over your cake. Yum.

Runny chocolate

No runny — chocolate

BOILING AND EVAPORATING

As soup heats up in a saucepan, it eventually becomes so hot, the watery part of it boils. The boiling water joins the air and becomes a gas.

Even before the soup boils, some of the water on its surface will get hot enough to form a gas. It will evaporate into the air.

As the water boils or evaporates, it gradually leaves the saucepan, so the soup left behind becomes thicker.

CONDENSING

All this cooking in the kitchen has made the air really warm – much warmer than the window which is cooled by the air outside. As soon as warm air reaches the window, the watery part of it cools enough to form droplets of water again. This change from a gas to a liquid is called **condensing**.

FREEZING

If you can't finish your soup, you can always freeze the rest of it. The inside of your freezer is so cold, it turns the water in your soup into ice. You can store your soup as a solid, just like an ice lolly, until you're ready to heat it up again.

MIXING IT

You can do a lot with materials by heating them up or cooling them down. But you can do even more when you bring materials together.

MIXING

This is the easiest thing to do with two materials. When you make currant buns, for example, you might start by mixing together some flour and currants.

DISSOLVING

Solids aren't the only things that you can mix together. It's often handy to mix together a solid with a liquid. For instance, you may like to put sugar in your tea. When you do this, the sugar breaks up into pieces that are so tiny, they become invisible. The sugary water you are left with is called a **solution**.

Not everything can dissolve in water. When Steven made Zelda a cup of tea, he accidentally put in some grit. The tiny stones made the tea so crunchy, Zelda had to get rid of them by passing it through another tea strainer.

Sorry! I thought they were tea granules!

FASTER AND STRONGER

Have you ever tried to make jelly from jelly cubes?

Jelly dissolves quickly in hot water. It dissolves slowly in cold water. A solid will always dissolve faster in a liquid that's warmer.

Maybe you like your jelly really strong. Instead of putting one lot of jelly cubes into a single jug of water, you might put in two. If you put in too many jelly cubes, you'd get to the point where there's not enough water to make them dissolve. This is always a problem with solutions – so stop being greedy.

A solid will always dissolve faster with hotter liquid

START HERE . . .

BRAND NEW MATERIALS

Sometimes, when you mix things together, something amazing happens. You make a brand new material from the ingredients that you put in.

RAISING IT

Along with milk, a key ingredient in bun making is bicarbonate of soda. It doesn't taste very nice – but a teaspoon of it is essential to make the buns light and fluffy. That's because it combines with the milk to make some brand new substances. One of these is a gas called **carbon dioxide**.

The gas is held in by the rest of the stretchy bun mixture. That's why it makes lots of little bubbles inside the mixture. The gas inflates the bubbles, just like balloons.

IN REVERSE

It's easy to make mistakes in the kitchen – so what do you do when you want to backtrack?

Well, if you've simply mixed two things together, you're in luck. You can separate currants from flour, for instance, just by picking them out (sieving will do the job quicker).

Even solids can be separated from liquids if they're in a solution. All you have to do is heat the solution gently so the liquid boils or evaporates. You can get the salt out of salty water, for example, by heating it on a dish over a radiator. As the water evaporates, you're left with a dish of perfect little crystals of salt.

Things get more tricky if ingredients have made brand new substances. Often it's impossible to reverse changes like these to get back to your original stuff. There's no way, for example, that you can 'undo' a cake to get back to the original ingredients. When cake baking goes wrong, it's often easiest to throw it away and start again.

BURNING

Of course, it's always a disaster when you burn whatever you're cooking. This happens when food gets so hot, it combines with oxygen in air. The food and oxygen form a new material – stuff that's black and hard. The sooty mess that you're left with can never be undone. Burnt food is burnt for good.

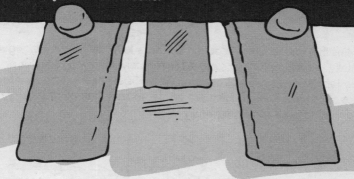

COLIN'S CHALKBOARD CONCLUSIONS

CHANGING STATE
Many substances will change state if you cool them
or heat them up.
Melting: turning a solid into a liquid
Freezing: turning a liquid into a solid
Boiling: turning a liquid into a gas
Condensing: turning a gas into a liquid
Evaporating: turning a liquid into a gas, even though it's not hot
enough to boil
MIXING
Some ingredients don't change in any way when you mix them
together. They can be separated out again easily. Other ingredients
combine when you mix them to make brand new materials. It's much harder
to 'undo' materials like these. Often, it's impossible.
SOLUTION
The mixture you end up with when a solid dissolves in a liquid (for
instance when sugar dissolves in tea). There's a limit to the amount of
solid you can dissolve in any liquid. In any liquid, there will be some
solids that you cannot dissolve.

IT'S ALIVE!

You've just found something big and hairy or small and slimy lurking in your bathroom. You want to find out if it's alive. Do you:

A. ask it?

B. prod it?

or C. scientifically study it for signs of life?

Answers:

A. This *will work*. But unfortunately, only if the live thing is human, speaks your language and is prepared to answer what is really quite a stupid question. This is a *very small percentage* of living things.

B. Can also work. But very annoying. And a bad tactic for things which are stronger than you. Can be cruel, too, for tree frogs, for example.

It seems that you're left with option **C**. That's to study your mystery guest carefully, searching for signs of life. Fortunately, there's a checklist of seven jobs that living things can do. We've listed them on the next few pages. Although some of them are harder to spot than others, they're a good way to tell if something really is alive.

If you study any guest long enough, you may find out if it's dead or alive. You may even grow to like it, and form a long-term relationship.

So, look for the seven jobs of life.

JOB 1: NUTRITION

Don't panic! This isn't complicated. Nutrition is just a fancy name for something we all love doing – topping up our body's supply of fuel and spare parts.

nutrition

Just like a car, your body needs fuel. It also needs materials to patch things up. These both come from the food you eat.

You have to chew the food you eat into smaller pieces. They are then turned into a mush so your body can soak up all the useful parts. This job, which goes on inside your body, is called 'digestion'.

DIET
Your body takes useful parts from your food to grow and patch itself up. So it's true that you are what you eat.

Your body does such a huge variety of jobs, it needs all sorts of ingredients. That's why it's important to eat a variety of food. Fresh fruit and vegetables, in particular, may contain lots of special bits and pieces that would be hard to find in any other food.

PLANT FOOD

All animals take in food, just like us – but what about plants? They can't exactly pop out for a takeaway, can they? And they're rubbish at chasing things.

Amazingly, plants make their own food. They put it together from very simple ingredients, with the help of some energy from the Sun. The main ingredients are water and salts which they soak up from the soil. To these, they add a gas called carbon dioxide that they take out of the air or water around them. These ingredients may not sound like a feast – but when sunlight shines on them, a plant can turn them into all the fuel and spare parts that it needs.

Leaves are big and flat, so lots of sunlight can reach them. Their green colour helps them to soak up the Sun's rays.

MISSING INGREDIENT

Which one of the following plants will be able to feed? Why will each of the others have problems surviving?

1. Plant with no soil

2. Plant in a dark cupboard

3. Healthy plant in soil and sunlight

4. Plant with leaves chopped off

5. Healthy plant in soil and sunlight, covered in tight plastic bag

JOB 2: GROWTH

Have you noticed something that all babies have in common?
Apart from the fact they smell, and dribble, and make otherwise
normal people say "Cooo-cooo" and pull odd faces?
Well, they're small.

And you're bigger. And heavier. The thing is, over a lifetime, all
living things get bigger. This is called 'growth'. The raw materials
for an animal's new body parts comes from the food it eats.

As you know, a plant makes its own food and uses this to grow.

You stop growing taller by the time you're in your twenties, but
your hair and nails continue growing all your life.

Almost all the raw materials needed to turn this tiny acorn into an
oak tree came from the soil and the air.

acorn +
soil +
air +
time =
―――――
tree

Clever, eh?

INTO SHAPE

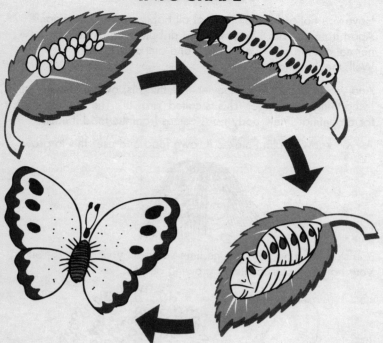

Some animals change shape completely when they grow.

For instance, when this caterpillar is fully grown, it makes a sack called a chrysalis. It crawls inside the chrysalis and stays there, changing its body shape. A few weeks later, it leaves the chrysalis, transformed into a beautiful butterfly.

LONG NAILS

On average, fingernails grow 2 millimetres longer each month. If you never cut your nails or let them wear away, they'd grow a metre long in fifty years.

Scientifically true but disgusting fact

If you didn't cut your nails, therefore, they would grow so long that you couldn't pick your own nose.

You could pick someone else's – and from quite a long way away, too. But that is another story. Which we are not allowed to tell you until you have a sick bag handy.

JOB 3: MOVEMENT

You know that humans, leopards, fleas and countless other animals move around. But did you know that even animals like these barnacles can move?

There are lots of different reasons for animal movement. Most animals move to find food, for example, or to go to places that are warmer, cooler or safer. Barnacles, for instance, waft the soft parts of their bodies to trap tiny sea creatures that they can eat.

Animals are constantly moving on the inside too. Your heart moves all the time, for example, to pump blood around your body. When your digestive system moves, it helps to churn up your food and squeeze it through your body.

Use it, or look like a tub of lard.

The more you gently move and stretch your body, the stronger and more supple it becomes.

Brian the ballet dancer bends and stretches many hours every day, so he is strong and supple all over. His body is really lean because all the energy-giving part of his food is used to keep him going during his long day of dancing.

Brian's brother Ben works at a desk all day and spends his evenings in front of the TV. He's not half as strong as Brian – although he's almost twice the weight. That's because he eats as much as Brian but is far less active. Unused energy-giving parts of his food are stored all over his body as fat.

IT'S ALIVE!

PLANTS ON THE MOVE

> But plants can't move, surely?

They don't take trips to the supermarket, but they really can move. Flowers in a garden, for instance, are rooted to the spot. Even so, they may open their petals when the Sun rises in the morning and close them when the Sun sets at night. They may also move gradually as they grow, for instance by leaning towards the sunniest part of the garden.

ANIMAL RACE

Can you put these animals in order of top speed, starting with the fastest?

cheetah

snail

human

ant

sloth

butterfly

snake

shark

goldfish

JOB 4: RESPIRATION

Keep calm! Breathe deeply! This one isn't as tricky as it sounds. In fact, plenty of respiration has been going on while you've been looking at this book.

So what exactly is this respiration that we've all been up to?

Well, think carefully about what you were doing when you were reading your book.

Um . . . I was scratching my nose, eating a sandwich and balancing on my rollerskates.

I was sitting quietly.

Yes, yes! But something else was happening too. You were also breathing. That's a job you have to do all the time, even when you're asleep.

Every time you breathe in, air fills two spongy sacks in your chest called your lungs. These soak up a fresh supply of oxygen, one of the gases in air. The oxygen passes from your lungs into your bloodstream so it can be sent to every part of your body.

QUICK EXPERIMENT TIME

Hold your breath.

Your body can't store very much oxygen. You need to keep breathing to top up your supply. If you hold your breath, you'll soon know that supplies are getting low.

So is respiration just another word for breathing?

Almost – but not quite. It's actually the name of the job you do with your supply of oxygen.

Your body is made up of millions of tiny working units called **cells**. These get their fuel from the food you eat (see page 81). Cells use oxygen to 'burn' their fuel so they can keep working. This is respiration.

Don't worry. Your cells don't make flames when they burn – but they do get a little hotter, so respiration also helps to keep your body warm.

Do all animals breathe, just like us?

Respiration is a job everything has to do – even animals that don't breathe in and out. Ants, for example, can't breathe. They don't have lungs.

But they do soak up oxygen from air that enters tiny tubes all over their bodies. Fish don't breathe like we do either. As they swim, their gills soak up oxygen from the water around it.

Ants and fish both use this oxygen in their cells during respiration.

What about plants then? I know they don't breathe.

You're right, they don't. But they still use oxygen to release energy from their food, just like animals do. So respiration happens in plants as well as animals. Plants soak up oxygen from the air or water around them.

This pot plant is in a plastic bag so it will soon run out of oxygen. When this happens, respiration will stop, so the plant will die.

JOB 5: EXCRETION

Just like a car or a sausage factory, all living things make waste when they work. Unless they get rid of this waste, it would slowly build up inside them and poison them. The job of getting rid of waste is called excretion.

When you go to the loo, your body is getting rid of two types of waste. Your urine (wee) is mainly made of waste salts and water from your body's working parts. Your faeces (poo) is mostly the parts of your solid food that your body didn't need. These solid parts passed all the way through your digestive system and out the other end. Your lungs help to get rid of waste too. Every time you breathe out, you get rid of water and carbon dioxide. These are waste products that are made during respiration (see page 87). They are carried to your lungs in your bloodstream.

QUICK EXPERIMENT

You can see the water that comes from your lungs if you breathe on to a glass.

Amazingly, even your skin works as a waste disposal unit. Salts and water leave your body through your skin every time you sweat.

COOLING DOWN

As sweat and urine both take some of your body's heat away with them, they help you to cool down. That's why most people sweat or urinate more on hot days. An adult who is exercising hard can lose up to 7 litres of sweat on a very hot day. That's enough to fill 21 fizzy drink cans.

Of course, animals produce waste just like humans, but their waste disposal systems don't all work in the same way. Worms, for instance, leave a trail of waste behind them as they burrow through soil. Although the way they do it isn't obvious, plants have to get rid of waste too. Plants make their own food so they don't have to get rid of food waste at all. They do need to get rid of water and carbon dioxide though. These leftovers from respiration drift out of fine openings in a green plant's leaves.

SMELLY ARMPITS

Amazingly, sweat doesn't smell 'sweaty' at all. It only starts to pong when lots of germs under your armpits feed on it, making a smelly waste of their own. The longer you leave sweat on your body, the more germs will feed on it, so the smellier it will become.

JOB 6: REPRODUCTION

Sadly, one day, your hamster will die. The same fate awaits your favourite pot plant, your friend's pet rabbit and that fly on the wall. Eventually, everyone you know will be dead, so will their pets, so will the plants in their gardens, and so will you. Nothing lives forever. That's why every species (type) of living thing has to make more of itself. This job is called **reproduction**.

Some living things reproduce much faster than others.

MOTHER, FATHER AND BABY

Eventually turns into adult

Gives birth to

Gets spots, turns into sulky teenager

Grows into sweet, innocent, happy child

It takes around 15 years, for example, for humans to develop enough to make babies. They usually make one baby at a time (two if they have twins). Most human babies are cared for by adults for a very long time – until they are well into their teens.

DOG, BITCH AND PUPPIES

Dogs, on the other hand, are ready to make pups by the time they are around nine months old. They can produce litters of twelve or more pups. These are ready to leave home within around eight weeks.

Simpler living things, like these germs, do not come in male and female forms. A single one can produce offspring all by itself. In just a day, one 'E. coli' germ can make millions of copies of itself. If these were in your dinner, they'd give you a bad dose of food poisoning.

10 minutes

YOUR BEDROOM

Half an hour

3 days

Plants use seeds to make copies of themselves. These can be carried far and wide by animals or by the wind. When the seed of a plant reaches a place where it can develop, it grows two shoots. One shoot grows downwards to make the plant's roots. The other grows upwards to make the plant's main stalk.

In fact, plants are sometimes pretty clever. If an animal eats an orange, including the pips, it will leave the pips in its faeces, so that the seed is surrounded by a handy supply of fertiliser.

Yes, but we like them so much, we grow them in enormous quantities. So, in a way, the seedless orange uses its popularity to make sure it gets reproduced.

But we've developed seedless oranges, haven't we?

JOB 7: SENSITIVITY

Colin has always been very sensitive. He's put lampshades on all the lights in his home because he doesn't like them too bright. When he hears a sudden noise, he jumps up into the air. In hot weather, he has to open all the windows but as soon as it gets chilly, he puts on his thermal vest.

You may find Colin's sensitivity a little tiresome – but sensitivity is something living things need to survive. If you see a tiger roaming the high street, for example, it's what will tell you to run away. All animals are sensitive in different ways. Cats, for example, like being stroked – but if you stroked a boa constrictor, you might get a nasty squeeze.

It's my fault, I'm so insensitive. Of course he didn't want stroking.

PLANTS

Okay, plants don't have feelings like we do – but they're sensitive, just like other living things. A plant will always grow towards the light, for example. On Earth, its roots will always grow downwards. That's because it's sensitive to the Earth's gravity. Imagine the problems with gardening in outer space!

EYES

Your body is sensitive in ways that you may not even know. When you see something really bright, for example, the black hole (pupil) in the middle of your eye shrinks to let in less light. The hole grows bigger when you are in dim light – or when you see someone you really, really like!

WHY DO PLANTS' ROOTS GROW DOWN?

Well, it's because over the years they've tended to find that it's more useful to get things from the soil and be stable in high winds.

Daffodil

Daft-o-dil (now extinct)

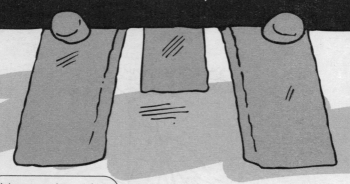

COLIN'S CHALKBOARD CONCLUSIONS

If you want to know if something is living, look for these seven signs of life:

1. Nutrition – taking in spare parts and fuel from food
2. Growing – making bigger body parts or growing new ones
3. Movement – for instance, moving towards food or moving somewhere cooler
4. Respiration – using oxygen in air to burn the fuel that makes a living thing work
5. Excretion – getting rid of waste and unused materials
6. Reproduction – making more living things
7. Sensitivity – noticing and responding to changes

You can breathe out now, Steven.

Phew!

GETTING ALONG

Yes, yes, we know you're very special. But you have to face facts. You're only one of around 8 billion people sharing this planet. Humans are only a small part of the picture. We're just one of millions of animal species that inhabit the Earth.

Then there are all the plants . . .

At the latest estimate, there could be up to 30 million different species alive on this planet. The vast majority of these have never been seen by a single living person. Together, they form a giant, living community.

Scientists call it a 'biosphere'. You can think of it as a very special kind of club.

Because hardly anyone is allowed to leave . . .

We all have to share the club facilities . . .

And even though individual membership of the club is for a limited time . . .

. . . if everyone keeps to the rules, almost all groups of members can survive.

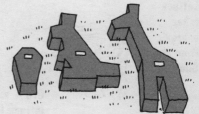

WHO'S FOR DINNER?

Don't fret over that tomato whose life was cut short for your ketchup.

MURDERER!

You're just acting out your place in the biosphere. You're part of a vast web of living things that have to eat each other to survive.

Some of us eat beefburgers, for example. They are mostly made of cows.

Cows themselves eat grass. You probably wouldn't eat grass yourself. Nor would you eat a tiger. But given half a chance, a tiger would eat you. It would also eat a cow. But it would prefer not to eat grass.

To see how living things depend on each other for food, it's helpful to write down a chain of things that eat others. This list, called a 'food chain', will always end up with a plant. A plant gets its energy directly from the Sun, so the Sun is the ultimate fuel supply for every living thing.

A simple food chain:

Dog eats chicken

Chicken eats grubs

Lettuce takes energy from the Sun

Grubs eat lettuce leaves

As very few animals eat only one type of food, it's helpful to link food chains together to form a food web.

A simple food web:

MAKE THE LINKS

Can you write out a food chain for each of these pieces of food? For example: sun – wheat – flour – human.

MADE UP SCIENTIFIC NON FACT

In a recently-discovered secret vault in an Egyptian pyramid, archaeologists have found a food chain diagram that has thrown into confusion many previously accepted theories of natural history. Here is the translated version.

Woovels eat themselves only and the species is now extinct.

HABITAT

What do you think of when you imagine a bear?

A brown bear that lives in the forests, a white polar bear living in the icy cold Arctic, or another type of bear altogether?

The two living bears share many features but have very important differences. These help each bear to survive in its own habitat (natural living place). For instance:

- White fur helps the polar bear to hide in snow and ice. A brown bear is better at hiding in the forest. Both bears need to hide so they can sneak up on their prey (the animals they will catch for dinner).

- The polar bear has much more fat than the brown bear. This helps it to trap more body heat so it can stay warm in icy weather.

- Unlike the brown bear, the polar bear has hairy paws. The hairs help it to grip on the ice.

Both bears were born with their special features. They help them to survive in their habitat. Imagine what would happen if you swapped them around.

SEE HOW IT'S SUITED

Bears aren't the only animals that are perfectly adapted to their habitat. Can you spot some of the ways that these animals have adapted too?

tall trees — long neck

Giraffe

long nose

Anteater

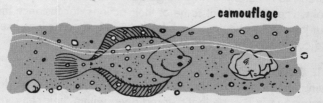

camouflage

Speckled plaice on the seabed

long tongue

Chameleon

INHERITANCE

Have you noticed how much children are like their parents?

Well, animals are like their parents too.

We say the looks of living things are inherited (passed down from parents to children). Living things don't only inherit their parents' looks. They also inherit some of their actions, for instance the way that they make shelter or look for food. Inherited actions like these are called **instincts**.

THE CODE

Living things inherit looks and instincts because they pass down this information in a code that's stored deep within their cells. The code is stored in a chemical called **DNA**. Chopping your arm off, changing your hairdo or losing your parents won't make any difference to this code. So events like these won't affect the instincts you pass on.

Inherited	Not inherited
A dog's fetching instinct.	A dog's broken paw.
A man's wiry hair.	A man's spiky hairdo.
A sheep's woolly coat.	A woman's woolly coat.
A fox's interest in catching rabbits.	Colin's interest in collecting stamps.

SOME INSTINCTS:

This rabbit burrows when it needs shelter.

This human cries when it is hungry.

This skunk makes a nasty smell when it is in danger.

Every one of these instincts is inherited. The animal does it naturally, without ever being taught. Some instincts aren't obvious straight away. For instance, the instinct that drives birds to make a nest only appears when they are ready to lay their own eggs.

HUMAN INSTINCT
Which of these activities do you think are human instincts? Which ones have to be learned?

sitting upright	tapestry making
driving a car	swimming
sucking	talking
urinating	playing the trumpet
flushing the toilet chain	using a knife and fork

GETTING ALONG

Imagine a pack of bears – all sorts of different shapes, sizes and colours. If they were living in the icy Arctic, which ones would be most likely to survive?

If you read page 98, you'll know that:

• The fattest bears will find it easiest to keep warm

• The palest ones will be best at sneaking up on their prey

• The ones with hairy paws will be the best at walking on ice

Fat, pale, hairy-pawed bears will survive the longest. They're the most likely ones to live long enough to make babies. Now their babies will inherit many of their features. They'll be fat, pale and hairy-pawed too. They'll have all the right features to survive even better in their habitat. As even more of them will live into adulthood, they will produce even more of the next generation of bears.

Every time a new generation is born, even more babies will show strong signs of these features. When they grow up, they themselves will have babies. As these will have inherited their features from their parents, these babies will be fatter, paler and hairier-pawed than ever.

Over millions of years, the bears will start to show such strong signs of these useful traits, they'll be perfectly adapted for the Arctic.

This way of adapting to a habitat over millions of years is called **evolution**.

The huge variety of living things on Earth all evolved like this. Amazingly, even humans and apes evolved from the same ancestors – ape-like creatures that lived millions of years ago. So apes are just like our very distant relatives.

Sometimes, when you go to the zoo, you feel that apes are not very distant relatives at all.

COLIN'S CHALKBOARD CONCLUSIONS

THE BIOSPHERE
Around 30 million species of plants, animals and other living things that all share planet Earth.

FOOD CHAIN
The way members of the biosphere eat each other to survive. Every food chain ends with a plant. This gets its energy from the Sun.

INHERITANCE
The way that features and instincts are passed down from generation to generation.

ADAPTATION
The way a type of animal or plant is made to suit its habitat (for instance, the way a polar bear is white so it can hide in the snow). Adaptation happens because the animal or plant with the best features are most likely to survive and reproduce.

Over millions of years, adaptation can lead to the evolution of entirely new species.

I suppose we can't all inherit the brains and good looks.

WHERE'S HOME?

Colin is writing a note to Zelda. Being an orderly person, he is careful to use his full address:

Colin
24 Stella Avenue
Manchester
Lancashire
United Kingdom
Europe
The World
Milky Way

Dear Zelda,

No room for news because of large address. Sorry.

Love, Colin

If you're planning to travel widely, then you'll need to know a bit about the world. Let's start with the easiest ways to travel from A to B . . .

TAKING A SHORTCUT

Steven and Zelda have been running into problems while they've been planning their next holiday.

To start with, they want to travel from Europe to Japan. Then they hope to catch sight of the reindeer in Canada. Finally, after a short stop at the sock factory in Iceland, they plan to go back home to the UK. Zelda has drawn their route on the map.

Oh dear. The journey looks so daunting – it's very, very long. Can you see a way to make it shorter? Well, they just have to remember that the world, unlike this map, isn't flat. It's actually like a giant ball.

When you remember that the world is spherical (ball-shaped), you can see it's only a short hop from Japan to Canada. That's if you travel east. At last! Steven's got the idea. His new holiday route is much shorter.

I DON'T BELIEVE IT!
Know your place!
It took thousands of years for explorers to draw a full picture of the globe. In the 1300s, European sailors had never seen the Americas but they had a hunch that a giant, unknown continent must lie somewhere in the ocean between Africa and Asia. But they knew little more about the size and shape of this continent than the ancient Greeks.

Well, since then, a lot of water has passed under the bridge. In 1492 Columbus sailed from Spain to America, tourists have been globetrotting and astronauts have taken photographs of the Earth from space. Most people accept that the world is spherical even if they haven't been all the way round it themselves.

However, just in case you are in any doubt that the world is a giant ball, here's some evidence:

Exhibit 1: Ship in the distance
Next time you're at the seaside, watch a ship going over the horizon. It will seem to disappear into the water as it sails out of sight. That's because it's travelling along the curved Earth.

Exhibit 2: Out of an aeroplane window
If you're lucky enough to travel somewhere by plane, take a good look out of the window. On a clear day, you should be able to see the curve of the horizon.

Exhibit 3: Space snaps
Photos taken from space clearly show that the Earth is a sphere. In 1968, the world was awestruck by the first ever space photos. They were taken by astronauts on their way to the Moon.

HOLIDAY PLANNING

Look at these five holiday destinations. Can you find a short air route between them?

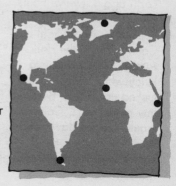

HOW BIG?
The Earth is a very big sphere – it's about 12750 kilometres in diameter. The Sun is spherical too but its diameter is 109 times bigger than the Earth's. Think of it this way: if the Sun was the size of a watermelon, the Earth would be as tiny as one of its pips.

IN A SPIN

Colin is a devoted nephew but finds it troublesome ringing his auntie. That's because she lives on the other side of the world. When Colin is eating his lunch, his auntie is tucked up in bed. That's not because she needs more beauty sleep than Colin. It's because her home is in the dark.

Zelda's holiday snaps may help to explain what's going on.

It was midday at Colin's when Zelda took this photo. The place on Earth where he lives was pointing towards the Sun. This meant his home was bathed in sunlight. Meanwhile, no sunlight was reaching auntie's house at all. For auntie, it was the middle of the night.

Of course, auntie didn't have to stay in darkness forever. The Earth is continually turning, bringing different parts into the Sun. Within a few hours, auntie's place turned into the sunlight so auntie saw the dawn. Meanwhile, Colin's turned away from the sunlight so he saw the sunset.

The Earth takes around 24 hours to complete one turn. That's the length of our day.

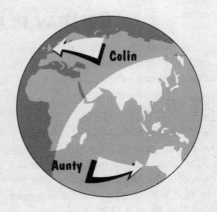

Zelda took this snap when she went past the Earth again, twelve hours later. This time, auntie's house was in daylight but Colin's was in the dark. Auntie was tucking into lunch while Colin was tucked up in bed. But in a few more hours, Colin would see the dawn and auntie would see the sunset again.

TIME ZONES

So no one has to eat their lunch in the dark, people around the world set their watches to different times. This map shows how people set their clocks in different parts of the world. The strips on the map are called time zones. People who live in each time zone set their clocks to the same time. The clocks show you how many hours they are ahead or behind the strip that's labelled GMT.

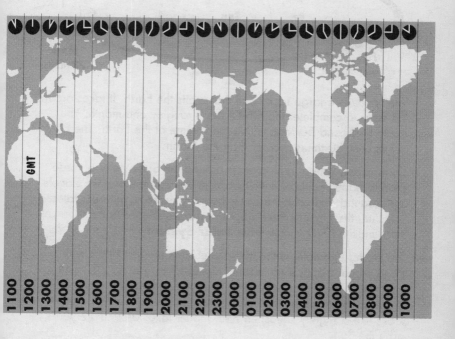

In the winter, everyone in the UK sets their watches to GMT. In the summer, they set them an hour ahead of this. This lets them enjoy warm summer evenings until later in the day (remember, if the clocks go forward, sunset will happen at a later time).

IN ORBIT

As well as spinning around, the Earth moves continually around the Sun. The path that it takes is called an **orbit**. It takes around 1 year for the Earth to complete one orbit of the Sun.

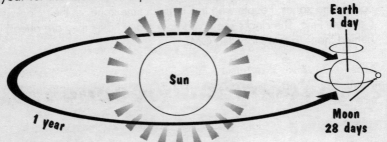

The Moon is a large rocky ball that orbits the Earth. It takes around 28 days to complete one orbit – that's roughly one month. You could fit around 50 Moons into the volume of the Earth. The Earth is just over 80 times heavier than the Moon.

Earth is only one of nine planets around the Sun. Many of these planets have moons of their own. Just like Earth, the other planets spin around and orbit the Sun – but they do so at different rates. The Sun, the planets, their moons and everything else that surrounds the Sun is called the **Solar System**.

Jupiter, for example, is the fifth planet from the Sun. It's a very large planet that has 16 moons. Jupiter takes around 10 hours to turn once. This is fast enough to force the middle of the planet outwards, just like the clothes in a tumble dryer. That's why Jupiter looks like a slightly squashed ball. Jupiter takes around 12 years to orbit the Sun.

GALAXIES

A few of the brightest lights in the night sky are planets. Almost all the rest are stars.

Stars aren't scattered evenly throughout the sky. They are grouped together in clusters called galaxies. Our own Sun is a star – one of 100 billion that form a galaxy called the **Milky Way**. You can see some of the rest of the Milky Way as a giant smudge of stars in the sky.

Around the Milky Way are countless other galaxies of stars. Any one of these could have a solar system of its own, including planets that may be teeming with life.

COLIN'S CHALKBOARD CONCLUSIONS

The Earth, Moon and Sun are all spherical.

The spinning of the Earth gives us our night and day.

The Earth takes exactly 1 day to spin around once.

It takes 1 year to orbit the Sun.

The Moon orbits the Earth once every 28 days.

The Earth is one of nine planets in the solar system, all of which spin around and orbit the Sun.

Our Sun is a star. It's one of 100 billion stars that form a galaxy called the Milky Way.

USER GUIDE

IMPORTANT ADVICE FOR ALL READERS – WHERE TO USE THIS BOOK

Congratulations on
a) purchasing the Science Repair Kit
b) getting all the way to page 113

The authors, illustrators, editors and publishers of this book, along with their accountants, hairdressers, neighbours, friends and relatives, are really impressed.

They would also like to take this opportunity to thank you for spending so much time and money on this small – but not insignificant – literary offering.

USER GUIDE

By now, you should be aware that this book gives you a powerful body of knowledge that can assist you in many life-enhancing situations. However, in the interests of hygiene, health and safety, the authors and their associates would like to offer the following essential user guide.

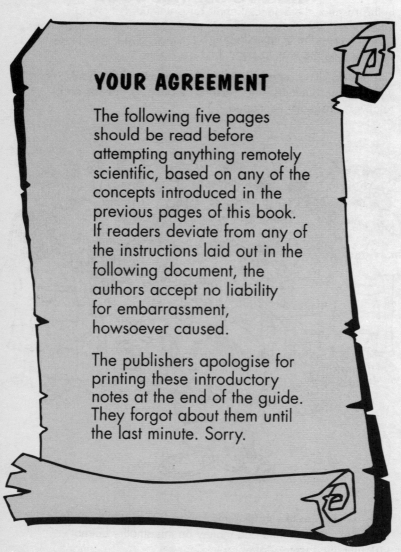

YOUR AGREEMENT

The following five pages should be read before attempting anything remotely scientific, based on any of the concepts introduced in the previous pages of this book. If readers deviate from any of the instructions laid out in the following document, the authors accept no liability for embarrassment, howsoever caused.

The publishers apologise for printing these introductory notes at the end of the guide. They forgot about them until the last minute. Sorry.

USER GUIDE: COUNTRIES OF APPLICATION

When you go to another country, the chances are you'll have to speak another language. Anyone visiting friends on the planet Zarg will also have to purchase another head.

In this respect, the Science Repair Kit is unique. Following laboratory tests, we were pleased to discover that its material was certified 100% scientific. This means it is accurate, useful and relevant wherever it is used – anywhere in the universe.

Keep chapter 2 handy, for instance, for any occasion when you need to work out speed and acceleration: on the road, underwater, or when travelling to friends on Zarg.

USER GUIDE: TROUBLESHOOTING

From time to time, you may find your personal experience of the universe does not exactly match your expectations after reading this book. We understand this can be disappointing.

When this happens . . .

- Stay calm

- Resist any urges to damage or deface this book

- Look for something obvious that you have done

- Look for something not so obvious that you have done

BustaBand – the only elastic bands with no stretch

- Remember: this is only a small book. We have only been able to scratch the surface of the science in our universe. While we have tried to give a true and accurate account of motion, forces, energy, materials and life on Earth, to the best of our knowledge, we have not been able to tell you everything there is to know.

That would have required a much bigger book.

Which would have taken far longer to write.

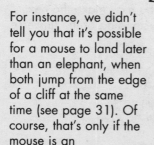

And cost a lot more money.

For instance, we didn't tell you that it's possible for a mouse to land later than an elephant, when both jump from the edge of a cliff at the same time (see page 31). Of course, that's only if the mouse is an accomplished skydiver.

USER GUIDE

- Cheer up! Some of the most exciting ideas were born when scientists noticed the world didn't match what others were telling them.

The great scientist Galileo caused a stir in the early 1600s when he insisted the Earth goes around the Sun. This idea had been around since the time of the ancient Greeks, and it was based on evidence – for instance, the way the stars and planets move across the sky. However, the Church at the time wanted people to believe the Earth was at the centre of the universe, and, although Galileo was right, he was forced to take back what he said and was put under house arrest until he died.

1642

NOTE: Please don't let this put you off a career in science. This was a long time ago. Scientists don't get treated so cruelly anymore. Well, hardly ever.

Thanks to the efforts of scientists like Galileo, we now take it for granted that the Earth is part of the Solar System. The Sun, at its centre, is one of billions of stars that make up a galaxy, which itself is one of countless galaxies in a vast universe. If you take a fresh look at your own experiences, you may make the next big discovery that will change our understanding of the universe we call home.

2006

WANT MORE?

Everyone has their own way of finding out more about science.
Here are a few methods other readers have recommended:

Dina

I find my local
science museum
amusing.

Bill

I explore the whole
universe from
my computer.

Zappa

I enjoy reading
about the unknown.

LIFE ON
EARTH
THE
EVIDENCE

If all else fails, try to enjoy your science lessons at school. If they're
too tedious, you can always spice them up by asking questions
about science that you think will fox your teacher (see page 6 for
some preliminary suggestions).

If this just makes your teacher mad, remind them that a good
question can spark the most exciting science in the universe.

CERTIFICATE

This is to certify that, whilst no one knows all there is to know about the world, with so much to be discovered, so much to be learnt, and seen, and understood, (what riches lie in wait!) – anyway, sorry, to certify that the following person now knows something, at least:

....

That only beauty therapists, poodle parlour attendants, fishmongers and actors in those really bad sci-fi films ever really wear white coats.

The Scientist's Union say: Here, here!

Glossary

absolute zero: A temperature of around 270°C below zero. Nothing in the universe can get colder than this.

air resistance: A force that makes it harder for things to travel through the air. Streamlined cars are designed to have less air resistance.

biosphere: The 30 million species of plants and animals that share planet Earth.

boiling: Changing from a liquid to a gas because something has become hot enough to reach 'boiling point'. Water boils to form a gas in the air.

brittle: A material is brittle if it breaks when you bend or twist it only slightly.

carbon dioxide: One of the gases in air. You put a lot of this gas into the air when you breathe out.

condensing: Changing from a gas to a liquid. Water in the air can condense on a cold window to form tiny water droplets.

conductor: A material that lets electricity or heat flow through it easily.

elastic: A material that springs back to its original shape and size after you stop stretching it.

energy: What you need to make things happen. Sound, light, heat, electricity are forms of energy. Things also have energy if they are on the move.

evolution: The way living things change, over hundreds of generations, because the ones most suited to their habitat survive long enough to have offspring (babies). For example, polar bears have evolved white fur so they can hide in the snow.

excretion: Getting rid of waste from the body. You excrete when you go to the loo, or when you sweat.

food chain: The way members of the biosphere (see above) eat each other to survive. You become part of the food chain every time you eat.

freezing: Changing from a liquid to a solid. When water freezes, it becomes ice.

friction: A force that makes it harder for things to slide or roll over each other. Friction between cycle tyres and the road, for example, gradually slows down cyclists when they stop peddling.

GLOSSARY

galaxy: A group of stars. Galaxies can contain billions of stars.

gravity: Something that exists between any two things that have mass, pulling them together. Gravity between you and Earth keeps you on the ground.

habitat: A living thing's surroundings.

inheritance: The way any living thing passes down looks, ways of acting and other characteristics to their offspring. You, for example, may have inherited your mother's hair colour.

insulator: A material that electricity and heat can hardly flow through at all.

mass: A measure of how much stuff something contains. Mass is measured in kilograms.

Milky Way: The galaxy that we live in.

nutrition: The fancy word for eating, in other words: taking in food to grow or repair the body and to keep it going.

orbit: The path of one object, turning around another in space. Earth, for example, is continuously orbiting the Sun.

reproduction: Making more living things. Your parents reproduced when they produced you.

respiration: Taking fresh gases into the body's cells and getting rid of waste gases. We take in oxygen and get rid of carbon dioxide by breathing in and out.

sensitivity: Noticing and responding to changes in your surroundings. You show sensitivity, for instance, when you blink in bright sunlight.

solar system: The Sun, the planets, their moons and everything else that immediately surrounds the Sun.

solution: A liquid and a solid that have mixed together so well, the solid has become invisible. Examples are jelly mixed with water and sugar mixed with milk.

tough: A material is tough if it needs lots of bending or twisting before it breaks.

weight: An object's weight is a measure of how much it is being forced downwards by gravity. Weight is measured in newtons. The weight of an object depends on where it is. You weigh six times more on Earth than on the Moon.

Answers

Page 15 Speed Challenge

Distance travelled	Time taken	Speed
10 kilometres	2 hours	5 km/h
15 centimetres	3 hours	5 cm/h
30 metres	10 seconds	3 m/s
16 metres	4 hours	4 m/h
12 kilometres	4 seconds	3 km/s
20 centimetres	5 seconds	4 cm/s
18 metres	3 hours	6 m/h
1 kilometre	1 second	1 km/s
24 kilometres	3 hours	8 km/h

Page 17 Pick the Winner
Car B has the most acceleration, but car C is the fastest. Car D has the broken accelerator.

Page 29 Newton Quiz
1. 125 N
2. 12 N
3. 5 kg

Page 35 Gravity Quiz
They **all** fall with an acceleration of 9.8 m/s/s.

Page 39 Weight Quiz

Animal	Mass	Weight on Earth	Weight on Moon
Rabbit	1 kg	9.8 N	1.6 N
Dog	6 kg	59 N	9.6 N
Polar bear	750 kg	7350 N	1200 N
Elephant	2000 kg	19600 N	3200 N

Page 46 Hot and Cold Quiz
Colin's armpit: 38°C
cup of tea: 70°C
inside of a freezer: 4°C below zero
coldest air at the South Pole: 60°C below zero
water inside a boiling kettle: 100°C
core of the Sun: 15 600 000°C
air in Zelda's flat: 18°C

ANSWERS

air inside an oven: 300°C
coldest temperature anywhere in the universe: 273°C below zero

Page 52 Electric Quiz

kettle: heat
food mixer: sound, moving energy
lawnmower: sound, moving energy

torch: light (and a little heat)
TV: sound and light
telephone: sound

Page 58 Lightbulb Quiz
Circuit A will make its bulb glow brighter than any one bulb in B
or C.

Page 60 Circuit Training

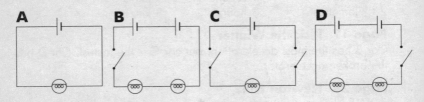

Circuits B and D are the same.

Page 68 Burning Question
Steven will burn his hand in situations A, C and D.

Page 70 Solid, Liquid or Gas?

puddle: liquid
spoon: solid
air: gas
bad breath: gas

soup: liquid
sweat: liquid
plasticine: solid
honey: thick liquid – or runny solid

Page 82 Missing Ingredient
1. This plant will have problems surviving because it has no soil
   from which to source water or salts.
2. The plant in the dark cupboard will have problems surviving
   because it won't have access to sunshine.
3. This healthy plant in soil and sunshine will be able to survive.
4. This plant will have problems surviving – without leaves it cannot
   capture the sunlight.
5. This plant will have problems surviving because it won't be
   able to get as much sunlight and it will soon run out of
   carbon dioxide.

Page 86 Animal Race

1. cheetah
2. shark
3. human
4. goldfish
5. butterfly
6. snake
7. sloth
8. ant
9. snail

This is the likely outcome, although it does depend on each of the creatures concerned.

Page 97 Make the Links

Lamb chops (sun – grass – sheep – human)
Bread (sun – wheat – flour – human)
Milk (sun – grass – cow – human)
Eggs (sun – corn – chicken – egg – human)
Kippers (sun – plankton – herring – human)
Honey (sun – nectar – bees – human)

Page 101 Human Instinct

Human instinct: sitting upright, sucking, urinating, talking.
Learned: driving a car, flushing the toilet chain, tapestry making, swimming, playing the trumpet, using a knife and fork.

Page 107 Holiday Planning

One short air route would be to start in Greenland (1) and fly over the poles to reach South America (2). From there to Mexico (3) and a flight around the globe ('behind' the map) to the east coast of Africa (4), and then on to the west coast of Africa (5).

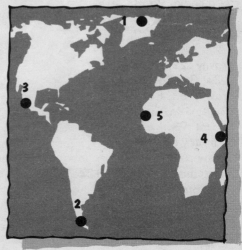

Index

ORDER FORM

0 340 89336 2	Grammar Repair Kit	£4.99	☐
0 340 91835 7	Maths Repair Kit	£4.99	☐
0 340 89334 6	Punctuation Repair Kit	£4.99	☐
0 340 91833 0	Science Repair Kit	£4.99	☐
0 340 89335 4	Spelling Repair Kit	£4.99	☐
0 340 91834 9	Vocabulary Repair Kit	£4.99	☐

Turn the page to find out how to order these books.

ORDER FORM

Books in this series are available at your local bookshop, or can be ordered direct from the publisher. A complete list of titles is given on the previous page. Just tick the titles you would like and complete the details below. Prices and availability are subject to change without prior notice.

Please enclose a cheque or postal order made payable to Bookpoint Ltd, and send to: Hodder Children's Books, Cash Sales Dept, Bookpoint, 130 Milton Park, Abingdon, Oxon OX14 4SB. Email address: UK.orders@bookpoint.co.uk

If you would prefer to pay by credit card, our call centre team would be delighted to take your order by telephone. Our direct line is 01235 400414 (lines open 9.00 am – 5.00 pm, Monday to Friday; 24 hour message answering service). Alternatively, you can send a fax on 01235 400454.

Title ...... First name .... Surname ....

Address ....

....

....

Daytime tel .... Postcode ....

If you would prefer to post a credit card order, please complete the following:

Please debit my Visa/Access/Diners Card/American Express (delete as applicable) card number:

Signature .... Expiry Date ....

If you would NOT like to receive further information on our products, please tick ☐.